RELEVANCE

RELEVANCE

The Power to Change
Minds and Behavior—and
Keep You Ahead of
the Competition

ANDREA COVILLE,
Chief Executive Officer, Brodeur Partners
with **PAUL B. BROWN**

bibliomotion
books + media

First published by Bibliomotion, Inc.
33 Manchester Road
Brookline, MA 02446
Tel: 617-934-2427
www.bibliomotion.com

Printed in the United States of America

Library of Congress Cataloging-in-Publication Data

Coville, Andrea.
    Relevance : the power to change minds and behavior and keep you ahead of the competition / by Andrea Coville, Chief Executive Officer, Brodeur Partners ; with Paul B. Brown. — First Edition.
        pages cm
    Includes index.
    ISBN 978-1-937134-82-2 (hardcover : alk. paper) —
ISBN 978-1-937134-83-9 (ebook) — ISBN 978-1-937134-84-6 (enhanced ebook)
    1. Competition.   2. Meaning (Psychology)—Social aspects.
3. Consumer behavior.   I. Title.
    HD41.C685 2014
    659.2—dc23
                                                    2013043688

To John Brodeur, for your support and validation of my original idea and for creating the momentum that got this all started. You believed a book needed to be written and so began the journey.

Contents

Contents

Acknowledgments

To Paul, my writing partner, who made the process of writing my first book the most humorous and fun creative collaboration I could imagine.

To Jerry Johnson, my partner in research for conducting the studies that supported the Relevance hypothesis. His knack for finding the insight that needed to be tested has been invaluable—not to mention his patience throughout the process.

I would also like to thank Rob Gould for creating what we affectionately refer to as the Relevance Egg, and his inputs into making it a diagnostic platform for communications planning.

Finally, to Bink Garrison, who early on pushed me to validate the concept of Relevance beyond my initial instinct.

Executive Summary

Organizations like yours spend, in total, billions of dollars annually to get people to buy a product, embrace a brand, follow a candidate, or join a cause. And yet we can all agree that these marketing campaigns, ads, public relations initiatives, communication programs, and social media and change efforts are—to be kind—often less effective than they could be. If you are honest, you'll admit you need help forging a lasting bond with the people you hope to influence.

To create that bond, organizations need a single, reliable guiding principle to ensure that all their marketing and communications efforts make a sustained impact. We are going to offer you one in the pages ahead. It can be summed up in a single word: relevance.

Merriam-Webster Dictionary defines relevance as "being practical and especially social applicability." And we think that's right, although we have found most people misread the definition, putting almost all their emphasis on the practical. That's understandable. It is certainly true that what you are offering must solve a customer need and do it well.

But increasingly, that is not enough. Customers are

becoming progressively fickle, as well as spoiled. They expect superior execution on your part. That is the price of entry, and, unfortunately, it's not something that will guarantee a long-term relationship. A slip on your part or a customer's encounter with a competitor that does what you do slightly better, or just as well at a lower price, and your customer may well abandon you.

And that is where the emotional part of relevance comes in. If your product/service/idea resonates with a customer, if it means something to him in addition to being utilitarian, then the relationship will be deeper, longer lasting, and more profitable. For example, value and dependability are the bedrocks of the ideal shopping experience. So providing those two things are absolutely necessary, but they give you no competitive advantage, because the other companies battling with you to gain market share are providing them as well. If all you do is what everybody else does you'll never gain an edge.

But, generation Y shoppers, according to our research, are much more likely—twice as likely as boomers, in fact—to say their favorite retailer delivers an experience that they'd like to share. The "shareability" component underscores the new social experience this cohort is looking for both offline and online. It's what is required to be relevant to them.

Relevance is the most important quality a brand, store, or experience can offer.

2

This is why relevance is so important. Unlike other objectives marketers have aspired to—engagement, "eyeballs," alignment, buzzes, clicks, and stickiness, for example—relevance has the power to change both minds and *behavior*. Those gen Y shoppers, for example, are going to search out retailers that provide experiences they want to share, leaving behind the ones that don't.

LOOK AT IT ANOTHER WAY

Here's another reason why relevance is so important. You can't get people to do things if they don't hear you. Sure, you can keep raising the volume on what you have to say to the point where people know you are trying to communicate with them. But the only way they are going to pay attention is if you can create an emotional connection. What you have to say needs to resonate. Your message must be personal if you want your audience to consider seriously what you have to say.

The connection also explains why customers will stay with you. It is easy for them to switch to another brand, and your customers will unless they feel some sort of personal connection to your offering. What's clear from both these situations is that relevance brings power, depth, and sustainability to the relationships we all have with companies, brands, and causes.

Unfortunately, many organizations have no idea whether they are relevant. Worse, they have no way to find out.

We are going to spend our time together examining

relevance in all its complexity and outlining ways to generate and, ultimately, sustain it. By the time we are finished you will understand not only what a powerful concept relevance is, but also how you can use it to leverage—perhaps exponentially—every part of your communications efforts.

Let's begin by talking about why it is so important.

THAT WAS THEN, THIS IS NOW

The world used to be a simpler place. Organizations offering a product, candidate, or cause were in the driver's seat. People had far fewer choices than they have today. And that was true whether you were talking about the type of wine you wanted to buy or where you wanted to get your news, and everything in between. If an organization had a good story or product or service, that was typically enough to earn a sale, vote, or commitment to a cause.

No one would describe the world as simple today. It's complex. Organizations face a new and daunting challenge: the people they are trying to reach are constantly bombarded with commercial messages that have made them cynical (to say nothing of the fact that they simply don't have the time to pay attention to more than a handful). Consumers have an expanding universe of options and new ways to select them. There are terabytes of information at their fingertips and networks upon networks to help them discover their friends' preferences and experiences with the things they are considering.

HOW AN OLD IDEA BECAME MEANINGFUL AGAIN

The increasing speed at which we all operate in today's world explains why an old concept like relevance is suddenly so important.

We used to take things for granted: if we were in business today, we would be in business tomorrow; someone who became a customer would stay a customer.

In the past, we could assume we were relevant by definition. As we have all learned the hard way, those assumptions are no longer true.

Today, you need to make yourself relevant to your customers or you will not be in business tomorrow.

You are either relevant—or you are history.

As attention spans shrink, messages, channels, and touch points are proliferating. Organizations need a reliable way to communicate effectively in this complicated new world, a way that is agile enough to adapt to dynamic conditions without sacrificing who they are.

They need a way to connect to the customers they are trying to reach. Every product, brand, and cause presents an opportunity for connection, but what will a person choose? Facing a staggering range of alternatives, people will connect with what is most meaningful to them. What seems most important. What is most relevant.

Relevance, often overlooked and certainly undervalued (See "How an Old Idea Became Meaningful Again"), has emerged organically as an ideal guiding principle for

5

creating effective marketing programs in this new, unpredictable, much more complicated world we live in.

IT'S ABOUT MEANING

In simple terms, relevance is that which provides meaning in our lives. Relevance is the full experience of a product, brand, candidate, or cause that we can relate to; it's an experience that, as we have seen, not only changes minds but, importantly, changes behavior—and sustains that change. The new behavior could be buying a product, supporting a candidate, telling a friend about what you have discovered, donating to a charity, or losing weight.

> Relevance is the full experience of a product, brand, candidate, or cause that we can relate to.

Consider the first-year high school student who challenges her teacher: "How exactly is geometry relevant to my life?" Her grades suffer until she discovers the thrill of student robotics competitions, which reveal a promising career path. Suddenly, geometry has meaning. It comes in the form of the elation she feels building something wonderful with her own hands and participating, with her friends as teammates, in various science and math contests. Suddenly, geometry has become relevant. The new behavior is rededicating herself to learning the material.

The key to understanding relevance is knowing that it's

spawned by many factors beyond logic. For example, everyone knows on an intellectual level that smoking is harmful, but that information is irrelevant—or at least not relevant enough—to a person who relishes nicotine's calming effect, or whose friends and family smoke and who savors the earthy aroma of fresh tobacco, or who has long associated that first cup of coffee in the morning with a cigarette.

Because this point is so important, let's stay on it for one more minute.

ARE YOU CONCENTRATING ON THE WRONG THING?

According to research conducted by Brodeur Partners caring for family and friends is the most important thing to Americans, by an overwhelming margin. Product marketers often get carried away with elements like features and "useability," while lifestyle promoters get caught up in the zeitgeist of self-discovery and meaning. But what both need to remember is that what people most value is how a product or service fits with their desire to nurture their friends and family.

> The near-universal aspiration toward compassion can say a lot about what and how people make sense of what is relevant in their lives.

A smartphone is good when it's fast and thin and has lots of apps—and better when it connects kids and parents across an ocean. A luxury car is a nice way to trumpet your status as you travel—and even better when your children receive the best protection available as your family moves from point A to point B. Security software is great when it prevents loss of valuable data—even better when it keeps companies afloat so employees can feed their families.

Within every product, brand, idea, candidate, or cause are human beings, families, and narratives to wrap around them. Find these people. Tell these stories. And, for maximum relevance in your communications initiatives, speak to people's deepest concerns.

Relevance may not be the first concept that comes to mind when considering a marketing program, but maybe it should be. Though imbued with new meaning for a new era of communications, it's a serious, sober word that speaks to the importance of deep, ongoing, honest relationships— meaningful commitments to products, brands, and ideas sufficient to change behavior.

THE THREE DIMENSIONS OF RELEVANCE

How do you go about building those meaningful commitments? There are three different ways. You need to employ all three, and we will discuss each in detail in the pages ahead, but here's a foreshadowing:

1. Segment

You cannot be all things to all people. But you can be relevant to all people based on some aspect of your offering.

You can find out which one will resonate by dividing your marketing by very specific categories: age, income, gender, education, geography, life experience, interests, politics, whatever, and determine how you can make what you have relevant to people in each of those categories.

Take the "simple" matter of buying eggs. It used to be that people had a choice of white or brown. Today, you can segment your sales differently. Are the eggs organic? Are they local? Are they freshly laid? By free-range hens? By hens that are naturally fed? Is the package made of paper or foam? Is it recyclable? Is it recycled or from virgin stock?

Today, the packaging material might be the trigger that prompts the sale. Yesterday, it was the mere availability of eggs on the store shelf. We are at a point where a simple purchase has more facets of meaning, and therefore, facets of potential relevance.

2. Intangibles

There are four components when it comes to building relevance. These four things, combined, affect consumers' responses to your offering, though often on a level they can't articulate.

Thinking. Clearly, cognition on the part of your audience may be necessary to create the change behavior you seek. You want them to logically consider the value of your offering.

Sensory appeal. How does the object you are selling look, feel, taste, smell, sound? This dimension can be overlooked, and it shouldn't be. Given two devices that perform equally well, surgeons will always pick the one that feels better in their hands. And, of course, users of Apple products rave about their appearance as well as their performance.

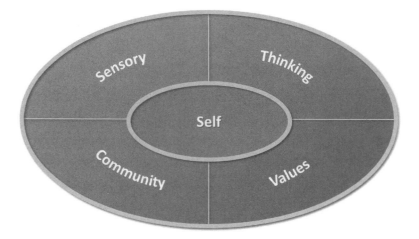

Community. The opinions of friends and respected advisers have always been important to consumers, and the Internet has made finding out what they think far easier than ever before.

Values. What is important to the person you are trying to reach?

Here's how these four components work in practice: imagine it's raining and you have no umbrella.

Thinking tells you that you need to buy one.

How does each umbrella feel in your hand? That's a sensory consideration every bit as important as the thinking. If the umbrella is awkward to use, you are going to end up getting wet.

Now, if everyone in your profession carries a black umbrella, you might not find relevance in a pink one with a unicorn on it. That's a community consideration.

So you want a black one, but which one? It may be important to you that the umbrella was designed with sustainability in mind, that it comes from a local retailer, or is the same brand your father and grandfather carried. These emotional elements reflect one's values.

3. Circumstances

Here we are talking about the relevance that occurs through content, context, and contact.

The *content* of a communication—say, words and pictures on a web page—is the primary vehicle for delivering relevance to an audience.

Context, by which we mean time and space, is another factor. What is relevant in the morning—a double espresso, for example—may not be relevant in the evening.

Contact is a third factor: relevance depends on the communication's source, be it a child, a doctor, a business (through a commericial message), or a political party, and it also depends on the medium itself. For example, communications experts are refining ways to spark online conversations and seed communities to trigger behavior. What was once an art is fast becoming a science.

One of the best ways we know to talk about circumstances is to talk about the antismoking "truth" campaign. For decades, antismoking activists warned teens that smoking kills. And teens kept smoking. Then a few smart adults sat down and got to know some teen smokers. The adults quickly learned—as parents everywhere already knew—that preaching at teens is the worst thing you can do.

Teen smoking is largely about rebellion.

Ironically, no institution is more "establishment" than the old-line, buttoned-up, manipulative tobacco industry. Thus was born "the truth" campaign, which shows teens the ways big tobacco tries to manipulate them.

That was relevant. The teens took the facts about the tobacco business in general, and the industry's marketing approaches in particular, and ran with them, rebelling against the tobacco companies. This response created a new social norm that smoking isn't cool. The National Institutes of Health cited the campaign as a major reason that in just one year, youth smokers declined by 300,000.

THE RELEVANCE CHALLENGE

Here are four things that are true, when it comes to relevance.

1. Relevance is more valuable today than it was yesterday. Here's why: choice has disrupted the conventional merchant–customer relationship. The consumer, rather than the retailer, is now in charge, since consumers have so many more options when it comes to where and what they buy. On top of that, organizations no longer know where their next competitor is coming from; it could come from down the block, or halfway around the world. As a result, there is both a greater need and a greater opportunity to be more relevant.

2. Relevance is more complex today than it was yesterday. Because people have more choices of products, services, and ideas—and more access to information about them—what is, and can be, more relevant increases. This is the crux of the relevance challenge. Fortunately, the technologies that have complicated relevance can also help us identify, draw out, and engage the people we are trying to reach.

3. Relevance is more difficult to establish today than it was yesterday. Thanks to technology, individuals now have an astonishing array of options in the marketplace as well as tools for evaluating them. And people have a greater ability to act on those choices. All they need to do is click on what they want, regardless of where it resides on the planet.

4. Relevance is more difficult to hold onto...because of the first three reasons.

WHY STAYING RELEVANT IS SO DIFFICULT

Remember, we are talking about relevance because of the impact it has in business. As businesspeople, we try to convert people into customers or supporters of what we do and retain them once we have convinced them. In short, we are trying to change—then maintain—their behavior.

It turns out there are five stages of behavior change: pre-contemplation, contemplation, preparation, action, and maintenance.[1]

Let's go back to our smoking example. In a study of people trying to change smoking habits, researchers found:

> Once in the contemplation stage, people were most likely to respond to feedback and education as sources of information about smoking. Preparation stage folks were committed to changing and seeking a plan of action. Those in the action and maintenance stages were actively changing their smoking behaviors and environments and found that social reinforcers were important. Those who had relapsed were found to cycle back into earlier stages as they geared up to quit again.[2]

Therefore, the message sent to early adopters of a product will vary from the one sent to laggards, just as the message sent to an energized political base will be different from that directed to the disaffected voter. In so many cases, it's not enough to have the right message. To be relevant, it must come from the right source and arrive at the right time to the right person in the right place.

THE RELEVANCE RISK

You understand implicitly the danger for an organization that simply assumes it is relevant. While it might see steady success today, its customers or constituents may be preparing to switch to other vendors or causes. Too often, organizations assume logic alone will prompt a desired behavior: a potential customer will switch to us because our offering is better. They fail to account for the full experience of emotions, senses, and social impulses.

CONCLUSION: ARE YOU RELEVANT?

As you have seen, relevance is a profound concept with major implications for any marketing program. In fact, it is probably your most urgent marketing imperative today, one we strongly suggest needs to be built into both your overarching strategy and your tactics.

Now that we've explored relevance—its definition, origins, dimensions, and implementation possibilities—only one question is left. How is relevance relevant? What is it about relevance that makes it a meaningful concept in a noisy world? What makes it worthy of an organization's full attention?

First, relevance focuses on results: the behavior change. Old-school concepts of awareness and engagement are the potential means, not the end. Relevance is about the ultimate goal—triggering the desired behavior.

Second, relevance is right for the times. The world has

moved beyond buzz, flash, glitz, shock, schlock, and deci-bels. It wants substance. It wants us to be relevant.

> It's time for authenticity, transparency, humility, mutual respect—and relevance.

That's why relevance needs to be part of your every offering.

People are awash in choices about where to spend their money and place their loyalty. If you aren't relevant, they will go somewhere else.

With all this by way of background, let's get to work.

1

Are You Relevant?

Why the Answer to That Question Is So Important

Even if you have never listened to *The Prairie Home Companion* on the radio, the name Lake Wobegon is likely to ring a bell. It's the fictional "little town that time forgot, and the decades cannot improve.... Where all the women are strong, all the men are good-looking, and all the children are above average."

In fact, this amusing description of this mythical place has spawned its own sociological term, the Lake Wobegon Effect, "a natural human tendency to overestimate one's capabilities." You can see it, probably most famously, when you ask people how well they drive. Just about everyone rates himself above average. If you have ever spent time on the 405 outside of Los Angeles or going through a Massachusetts rotary, you know that is simply not the case.

You can also see the Lake Wobegon Effect in full force when it comes to relevance. Ask someone where her product or service ranks on a relevance scale from one to ten, and the odds are that she is going to put it between six and nine. True, very few people will give their product a ten, but it is the rare person who will award his offering less than a five. And no one we have ever met has said "one," even though by definition 10 percent of the universe would have to be.

Why do people give themselves this higher (and probably inaccurate) rating?

Well, just like no mother has ever had an ugly baby, we humans have a tendency to see something we care about in the most flattering light. But it is more than that. We tend to look for confirmation of how well we (or our product or service) are doing among our friends, coworkers, and best customers and clients, and they are unlikely to tell us what we don't want to hear. That's just human nature. As is the fact that we tend to be tougher, but also more objective, when evaluating the competition. (And, of course, the lower the score we give them, the better we are going to look in comparison.)

WHY RELEVANCE?

We believe relevance is the new communications imperative. We live in an increasingly chaotic media environment with ever-shrinking attention spans and rising skepticism. In a multichannel world where people have more and more choices, making connections is not only more difficult, it is more important.

Then there is the whole matter of positioning. We are taught to place our product/service in a context where it appears best. You would never describe your tiny office supply store as "one of the 8,671 places nationwide where you can buy paper clips." You'd say, "We are the leading supplier of all your office needs on Main Street."

This means that if you work hard enough, and make your focus narrow enough, you can always define yourself as relevant. If we could find a maker of buggy whips, odds are he would point us to his very small list of customers and say he was relevant to them. And he would be right, even though he wouldn't be relevant to a great many people, including his banker.

Most of us want to reach a broader audience than those people who still use buggy whips—and that's a good thing.

But consider the people you are trying to reach. They are:

• **Receiving more messages than ever.** The estimates vary, but there is no doubt that the average person is subjected to thousands (five thousand seems to be the consensus) of commercial messages every day. And that is just commercial messages. That tally doesn't include mail—regular or e-mail—phone calls, memos, white papers, texts, IMs...

• **Having more people vying for their business.** Competition today can come from down the block or around the globe. More and more companies are battling for the attention of the same potential customers you are.

- **On tighter budgets.** No one ever had money to waste, but there is no doubt that budgets are more restrained than they have been. People are simply not going to waste time on messages for things they either can't afford or that have no meaning in their lives.

- **Pressed for time.** What's true for you is true for customers. Your potential clients are (extremely) time-pressed. Odds are, their company, like most, is trying to do more with fewer people. (If companies are not laying off employees, they are trying to keep head counts frozen, which means there are fewer people to do the same [or more] work.) And on top of that, everyone is trying to squeeze in a personal life.

- **Facing lots of competition for their time.** There is simply no downtime any more. Between twenty-four-hour news cycles, the ability to DVR television shows, and the fact that you can check your e-mail on your smartphone every fifteen seconds if you want, we are never "off." When people have several options for how they are going to spend every minute of every day, getting their attention is extremely difficult.

- **Not uniform in their makeup.** A slowing economy has created an incredibly interesting phenomenon. Employees at the company you are trying to sell to could be in their twenties or their seventies. One size definitely does not fit all as you develop a marketing approach to reach them.

- **The net result? They are becoming more demanding.** This isn't surprising given the work and the time pressure and the constant bombardment of messages your customers and potential customers receive.

And you have less time, too. So you only want to work on things that have the greatest impact. You want to leverage that impact wherever possible. A wonderful ad campaign that is irrelevant to your core audience simply is not a wonderful ad campaign. (If it doesn't increase awareness and revenues, you have failed, no matter how clever the spot was.)

RELEVANCE: THE RIGHT WORD
AT THE RIGHT TIME

"Relevance? Jheesh. Another buzz word," the skeptics cry. "I should just add this to 'engagement,' 'enlightenment,' 'eyeballs,' 'stickiness,' and the like and move on, right?"

We understand the reaction. In fact, we share it. We were so fed up with the buzzword du jour that when we went looking for a single word to describe what is needed in marketing today we went searching for an old one—and we found it in relevance.

"But aren't you going about it backward?" you may ask. "Isn't relevance a natural byproduct of taking care of your customers? If it is, then isn't all this talk about the importance of relevance really letting the proverbial tail wag the proverbial dog?"

It's a great question. And we think part of the point is right. Of course, you want to take care of your customers. But that is simply the price of entry. You have to do that to remain in business. And if we were to link taking care of your customers to the definition of relevance, it would go to the "practical" part in the definition, that relevance is *practical and especially social applicability.*

But your goal of being relevant should not be to do the minimum. You want to leverage all your actions and lead to a behavior change, whether it is ensuring that existing customers stay with you or that people you would like to become your customers do.

So, relevance turbocharges your desire to take care of your customer. Companies with high relevance scores appear to produce superior growth when compared with their peers. It is unclear whether the high scores lead to superior growth, or whether superior growth and performance create greater relevance. In any case, there is a clear correlation.

All this explains our starting point and underscores why relevance is so important. If what you are offering isn't relevant, nothing else matters. Your strategy is ruined, and so are your tactics. You want people to respond to your marketing initiatives. They won't if there is no reason to, that is, if your product or service is not relevant.

RELEVANCE AND STRATEGY

Professor Bernie Jaworski is the Peter F. Drucker Chair in Management and the Liberal Arts at the Drucker School at Claremont Graduate University.

Here is what he has to say about strategy and relevance (and the emphasis in the last point is ours):

Differentiated products, service, and business models only come from differentiated customer insights. A customer insight must pass four screens:

1. No one else has it and it is surprising.
2. You can act on it.
3. It can drive substantial growth.
4. **It is highly relevant to customers.**

"Okay," you say. "But why the focus on relevance now? After all, you were the first to admit that it is an old concept. Why is relevance worth my attention today?"

That's simple. With all the information that is coming at us all the time, we need a filter to help sort the stuff we won't pay attention to from the stuff we will. And relevance performs two vital functions in that respect.

First, it serves as a primary sorting device: "I'll pay attention to A but not to B, C, and D."

Second, it prioritizes the messages we are going to pay attention to. The more relevant the message, the higher it goes on the list.

So, if you are relevant:

1. Your message gets through.
2. If your message gets through, people will consider it.
3. If people consider it, they may do what you want.

WHAT DO PEOPLE SAY?

Here is one simple way to find out whether you are relevant or on your way there: listen to what people say when they describe your offering.

You want them to respond with words like these:

- I associate [the product or service] with values that are important to me.
- It stands for the same things I do.
- Being associated with it makes me feel better about myself.
- I want people to know that I am associated with it.
- It helps me meet my needs.
- It makes my life easier.
- It is not for everyone, but it is for people like me.
- It inspires me.

There are other benefits as well. For example, concentrating on relevance keeps you customer-focused. The needs of your customers change over time; if you are constantly ensuring that you remain relevant, you will change with them. Our maker of buggy whips may have become a manufacturer of after-market automobile accessories, had he been focused on remaining relevant.

MORE REASONS WHY OBTAINING RELEVANCE IS HARDER—AND MORE IMPORTANT

We talked earlier about why it is so difficult to get through to people. In addition to all the messages we receive and the time pressures we face—or maybe in part because of them—there is a large and growing amount of distrust. When was the last time you believed an ad or a salesperson you had never dealt with who said something was "the best" or was the "lowest price" or "highest quality"?

On top of that, it seems we are more anxious. We have always worried about our families, of course. But now, we need to worry about whether we will have a job tomorrow. And then there are the terrorist concerns that are always hovering in the background. We are concerned that our leaders have become progressively more ineffectual, meaning that, more and more, we are responsible for ourselves.

INCREASING POLITICAL POLARIZATION

It is not your imagination. The basic beliefs and values of Americans are more polarized than they have been at any point in the past twenty-five years, according to the nonpartisan Pew Research Center: "Unlike in 1987, when this series of surveys began, the values gap between Republicans and Democrats is now greater than gender, age, race or class divides. The average partisan gap has nearly doubled over this 25-year period."

(Continued)

25

Even worse, the people surveyed are deeply entrenched in their positions: "Both parties' bases have often been critical of their parties for not standing up for their traditional positions. Currently, 71% of Republicans and 58% of Democrats say their parties have not done a good job in this regard." If they had, the gap would have been even wider.

What is intriguing is that the other traditional divisions—gender, race, ethnicity, religion, and class—have remained the same. That makes the partisan divide much more striking.

According to the study:

In recent years, both parties have become smaller and more ideologically homogeneous. Republicans are dominated by self-described conservatives, while a smaller but growing number of Democrats call themselves liberals. Among Republicans, conservatives continue to outnumber moderates by about two-to-one.

The study found that "currently, 38% of Americans identify as independents, while 32% affiliate with the Democratic Party and 24% affiliate with the GOP." That is little changed from recent years, but, not surprisingly it seems to us, "long-term trends show that both parties have lost support."

No one—not even James Bond, Jason Bourne, or any other spy fictional or real—likes living in a state of continual mistrust.

All this suggests another reason that relevance is so important today: people want something to believe in, even if it is only a product or service that never lets them down. And if you can become relevant, the payoff can be huge. Specifically, six things happen, all of them good.

1. **Your sales go up.** People have a reason to do business with you.
2. **If you are helped (i.e., your sales go up), the competition is hurt.** If people are spending money with you, they are not spending that same money with the people you are competing against.
3. **They stay with you longer.** Acquiring customers is always an expensive undertaking. If you remain relevant to your existing customers, they have fewer reasons to leave you.
4. **The loyalty builds a barrier to competition.** If you have done a good job taking care of customers and remaining relevant, it is going to be difficult for your competition to lure them away.
5. **It is easier to get customers to buy more.** This is simply the flip side of the last point. It is always easier to sell additional products and services to people with whom you already have a good relationship.

6. **You can achieve higher margins**. If you do a good job taking care of your customers, they are willing to pay a bit more for what you offer. You can't gouge them, of course. But they will be a bit less price sensitive. Most people really do believe, as we do, that you get what you pay for.

HOW DO YOU BECOME RELEVANT?

Okay, you are convinced that relevance is a good thing. So, how do you do it? How do you become relevant? We devote the rest of the book to answering that question. But let's do a bit of foreshadowing. The following graphic will give you a clue.

As you can see, there are four ways you can be relevant. Let's take the categories one at a time and see what the person you are trying to connect with will say if your offering resonates with her.

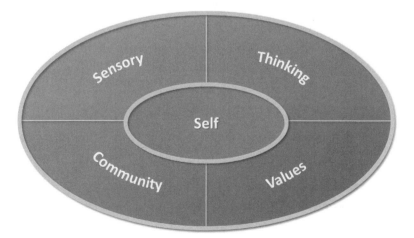

Thinking (Functional)

- This product/service helps me meet my needs.
- It makes my life easier.

Sensory appeal

- This product/service is part of my routine or habit.
- It just feels right.

Community

- Being associated with this product/service makes me feel better about myself.
- I want people to know I am associated with it.

Values

- I associate this product/service with principles that are important to me.
- It stands for the same things I do.

Given all this, you can see why relevance is so important. The question, of course, is how you can become relevant—and stay relevant.

That's where we turn our attention next.

TAKEAWAYS FROM CHAPTER 1

1. **You need to be relevant. Period.** Without relevance, no marketing initiative is going to get through, let alone resonate.
2. **Gaining relevance is harder than ever,** given all the messages out there and the time pressures we are all under.

3. **Because relevance is harder to achieve, it is more important.** Mastering relevance will give you a huge edge in the marketplace.

THINGS TO DO MONDAY MORNING

✓ Rate your product/service on the relevance scale from one to ten, one being completely irrelevant and ten being of utmost relevance.

✓ Ask others—especially your clients—to rate your offering on the same scale.

✓ Look at the disconnect (invariably, there will be one). Figure out how to close the gap.

Try this exercise to hammer home all of what we just discussed:

As you have seen, relevance deals with more than the rational; it also involves emotions and senses. With that in mind, think of something—a product, candidate, cause— that you are particularly attracted to and determine why that is the case.

How would you attach those same feelings/reasons to something that you (or your organization) currently sells?

2

Everything Is Personal

That Includes the Relationships
Your Customers Have with You

With the three words of our chapter title—"everything is personal"—you understand why relevance is so important. Want proof? You need look no further than the local Cineplex or the flat-screen television on your family room wall:

You have seen the scene a thousand times in the movies or on TV.

Two people have been working on a possible deal. Our hero desperately needs the agreement to save the farm; stave off bankruptcy; keep the bank from foreclosing; pay for grandma's operation; get funding for his BIG IDEA (which will allow him to win the girl), and he thinks he has convinced the other person— usually someone who already has a lot of money and/or power—to agree to terms.

Then, at the last minute, there is a phone call, a face-to-face meeting, a telegram, an e-mail, or a text that says, "The deal is off/I've changed my mind/I got a better offer."

No matter what form the communication takes, the message always ends the same way: "It's nothing personal. It's just business."

Every single time that scene plays out, you are rooting for—and ultimately feel bad for—the person who received the "it's just business" message. And that is true whether you are running a nonprofit or are the most flinty-eyed CPA who ever lived. No one watching *It's a Wonderful Life* roots for the hard-hearted Mr. Potter.

On the surface, this makes no sense. Shouldn't we identify with the person who gets the best deal, the one who comes out ahead?

Ah, you say. But we are talking about a movie or a television show. The people who create entertainment know how to play on our emotions. So, it is not surprising that we are rooting for the underdog. It's a standard plot device. And it is a standard plot device because it is so effective.

All that is true.

But it's a funny thing. For most of us, real life is a whole lot like reel life, at least in this regard: When people play the it's-nothing-personal-it's-just-business card with us we always feel worse than we should by any objective measure.

Why? Because we have invested time and probably a lot of emotion in the deal that has fallen apart. When we analyze the situation in retrospect, we see that we believed there was some sort of relationship, a connection with the person we were negotiating with that we thought went beyond business. When we find out there was no such connection, we feel disappointed, if not betrayed.

And these feelings get us back to the definition of relevance (which, as you'll recall, is "practical and especially social applicability"). If relevance was simply the first part of the definition—something that is practical—there would be no hard feelings. We were negotiating a deal and it didn't work out. The other person did, indeed, get a better offer and it just makes sense for her to go with terms superior to what we were proposing. These things happen. On to the next deal.

However, relevance is not just about the practical. It has a huge emotional component (that's the "especially social" part of the definition). And that's why the "it's just business" line stings so much, because, implicitly, we never thought it was just business.

But the converse is also true.

You wake up in the morning knowing that later that day you are going to pick up your college-age daughter who has just spent her Christmas break halfway around the world volunteering at a place you can barely find on a map. However, when you check your smart phone, you discover that, while you've slept, she has sent you an e-mail that says, "They cancelled our plane. And the next flight home won't be for three days. So, I am taking a flight that lands [at an airport 125 miles from your home] at 3 a.m. your time. If there is time, I'll call you from London when I am changing planes. Hope this is not a problem. Love you."

So, before you have your coffee you call the car service you always use—the one that is about 15 percent more expensive than the competition but which has never let you down—and ask them to pick up your little girl at 3 a.m. at that airport that is more than two hours away. The car service e-mails the confirmation to you, and you then forward it to your daughter so she can read it when she changes planes. She doesn't have to worry—and neither do you.

Much has been made about Americans' search for meaning and truth through self-exploration and spirituality. Research by Brodeur Partners shows that these things are actually relatively low on people's ratings of personal importance. Caring for friends and family, staying healthy, being in a loving relationship, and being financially secure dramatically outweighed finding meaning and being understood.

As you have breakfast with your daughter the following morning—just before she heads to bed for twelve hours of make-up sleep, you have this passing thought: "I guess I won't be changing car services any time soon." The car service has proven extremely relevant in your life. It took care of the thing most precious to you.

AND THEN THERE IS YOUR PERSONAL LIFE

These two stories—of the deal that's "just business" and the trustworthy car service—cover the spectrum when it comes to why everything is personal. To add another example, even though we call our work an occupation, we want it to have meaning. There is nothing more depressing than putting forty or fifty years into a job and thinking it hasn't meant a thing. So, of course, work is personal. If it isn't, there is something wrong.

Conversely, in our personal lives we have so many choices—from where we live to which cell phone we use—that we simply want what works best for us. You could say that makes us narcissistic. We'd simply say it makes us human.

So it turns out that staple of entertainment—the "it's just business" scene—is extremely entertaining, and just as equally wrong. It doesn't matter whether we are talking about the kind of pen we use or who we do business with, everything is personal.

TAKEAWAYS FROM CHAPTER 2

1. **Everything is indeed personal.** Everything. Need proof? Think back to the last time you lost a deal. Were you dispassionate? Rationally accepting? (We thought not.)
2. **Think of the flip side.** How do you feel when a difficult negotiation ends in your favor? You are not

rationally accepting then either, are you? It's another example of why everything is personal.

3. **As you negotiate going forward...**remember that you are going to take the deal personally and act accordingly.

THINGS TO DO MONDAY MORNING

✓ Talk to your customers about why they do business with you.

✓ Compile a list of the noneconomic reasons.

✓ Determine what you can do to capitalize on those strengths.

Try this exercise to hammer home what we just discussed:

Look around your office. Pick out an object you are really neutral about (your stapler, a paper clip, whatever). Write a paragraph about it, putting it in the best possible light you can.

Then, think of something you care about deeply. A cause. A loved one. An idea. A product. Write a paragraph about it.

We guarantee the second paragraph will be far better than the first. When you have a personal relationship with someone or something, it shows.

3

Dimensions of Relevance (I): Quantitative

One Size Does Not Fit All

Almost everyone thinks successful innovation starts with a great idea. Almost everyone is wrong.

The great idea comes second. You must begin with the killer insight, a deep truth significant enough that it helps you make a meaningful number of sales or allows you to forge relationships with a large number of people.

Ultimately, an insight tries to make someone's life simpler and more economical, profitable, efficient, and—if it is truly meaningful—worthwhile.

And the easiest way to come up with that insight, an idea that is going to resonate with your customers and potential customers (in addition to increasing sales, earnings, and market share), is to connect an attribute of your offering to a need your customers have. Then you must show how what you have come up with can make their lives better. More specifically, you want to demonstrate why at least some aspect of your offering solves a problem or fills a need that it is relevant to your customers.

Why is developing the insight the place to begin? That's simple. Insights are so important because ideas are so easy. We are convinced you could come up with twenty killer ideas before lunch—everything from making it possible to fly a jet to work to simplifying the tax code—if you really had to.

Coming up with ideas isn't a problem. But, ironically, starting with the idea—even if it is a great idea—can be. Why? Because if you start with an idea there is no guarantee you are going to connect with your target audience. You could come up with a solution for no known problem. Or for a problem your target customers simply don't have. Examples abound. Let's explore one briefly. The following example comes courtesy of Mike Maddock, who has written a wonderful book, *Brand New*, on the subject of innovation. That isn't surprising. Mike's company, Maddock Douglas, is one of the world's leading innovation consultantcies.

The Iridium phone was a truly great invention. We are guessing here, but we believe that the inspiration for the product was this:

Wouldn't it be great if we created a cell phone that allowed you to call or e-mail anyone in the world from anywhere in the world at any time? And by everywhere, we mean everywhere: the poles, oceans, sky, and absolutely everywhere in between.

Who wouldn't want a phone capable of delivering communications to and from the most remote areas in the world, where absolutely no other form of communication is available?

When you ask the question that way, the answer would be: of course everyone is going to want one.

But when you start giving people a bit more information ("the phones are going to cost what?!; and *"how* much a month?!"; and "the charge per minute is going to be *what?!)* you would quickly realize the number of people who want the phone *and are willing to pay for it* is not large enough to support the investment.

That's why you need to begin not with the idea but the insight that identifies what the market needs and is willing to pay for.

And when you do, your default position must be this: *you cannot be all things to all people.* Common sense tells you why.

First, it is virtually impossible to find a product that everyone needs. Water, you say. Okay. Tap? Naturally sparkling? Carbonated? Bottled? Branded? Imported? Single source? Flavored? With vitamins added? You get the idea. Even what seems like the world's most basic commodity, water, can—and has been—sliced and diced (if you can slice and dice water) into endless variations.

Second, you run the risk of looking ridiculous if you try to be all things to everyone. Think about people who don't dress age appropriately. It is not a pretty sight. It is no different when you twist yourself into a pretzel trying to make your state-of-the-art router seem appealing to everyone ("Grandparents will love it because...") or when you attempt to make that new boy band into a group for "music lovers of all ages."

Third, reaching the widest possible audience requires you to be extremely bland. You can't risk offending anyone for any conceivable reason as you search to lure every possible customer you can. And bland things are, by definition, commodities. There is no emotional connection to a commodity. (Don't believe us? How connected are you to tap water or white sneaker laces? They are commodities and don't offend anyone, unless there is some kind of flaw with them. But you are not fiercely loyal to them either.)

You can't be all things to all people and still be relevant. To be relevant you need to, as we said, find a need you can satisfy and then fulfill that need for a core audience. You build from there.

If you picture an archery target, you understand how this works.

You start with the bull's-eye in the exact center, and then move out to the next closet ring, then to the ring outside of that and so on. In other words, you start with your strongest core market and expand (slowly) from there.

A STRONG CORE CAN BE A HUGE NICHE

We believe passionately that the way to build relevance is to create a ridiculously loyal bunch of customers, users who serve as your foundation, and build up and out from there.

But you should only build off that base to the point where it makes sense. You can't be all things to all people, and the more you try, the more you will dilute the attractiveness of your offering.

Just about everyone concedes the logic of that, but then some people say, "By taking this approach are you dooming yourself to offering niche products?"

Our answer is, not necessarily. Fans of the *Star Wars* movies, Starbucks, and the STARZ cable channel are fiercely loyal—they provide a core audience for those three franchises, and collectively they number in the hundreds of millions.

But even if your core represents only a small part of the overall market in which you compete, it is still possible to make a lot of money.

(Continued)

Crocs, those odd-looking shoes, represent a minuscule portion of all the footwear sold annually. But sales of Crocs recently topped $1 billion a year. Apple only has 5 percent of the personal computer market, but the company is sitting on more than $100 billion in cash, as a result of the high-margin products it has been able to sell throughout the years. And comedian Louis Szekely, better known as Louie C.K., may have a cult following, but he has been able to bypass the traditional way of producing a comedy show and selling tickets. He charges $5 to see his show via computer, and, by all accounts, he is making a fortune from his relatively small but devoted following.

The point: a strong core can be hugely profitable.

Zipcar is one example that comes to mind when we think of starting with a core audience and expanding organically. The world was not crying out for another rental car company when Zipcar went into business in 1999. After all, Hertz was founded in 1918 and the "upstart" Avis began in 1946, so competing broadly would have made no sense. Between Alamo, Avis, Budget, Hertz, National, Thrifty, and the like, this was not exactly an underserved market. Instead of taking these competitors head on, Zipcar went after a niche: urban dwellers who don't own a car but could use one from time to time. From there the company expanded, first geographically (i.e., into different cities) and then by the people it targeted (it went from focusing on young urbanites to city dwellers of any age).

When we tell clients they need to start with a base and build from there, as Zipcar did, some object, saying, "If we only get 10 percent of the market, that leaves a 90 percent market share to someone else." Our answer is always the same, and it has two parts. First, no company is going to get 100 percent market share or close to it, unless it is a utility or another regulated monopoly, and if it is, the government is going to cap what it charges anyway. Second, your competitors are going to have the same problems you will if they try to be all things to all people—and it is not going to work for them either.

That's why you need to start with your core and build your way outward, as you work to become relevant.

THINKING UPSIDE DOWN

Is the converse true? Can you always find a way to be relevant to someone?

Yes. With a couple of provisos.

First, you can't make a terrible product or provide a lousy service. Things that fall apart or make our lives less appealing are never going to be relevant no matter how hard you try.

Second, when you are dealing with the very technical, or operating in a space that is extremely specialized, you simply may not be able to forge the emotional resonance you seek beyond an extremely small number of people. For example, physicists went absolutely gaga over the discovery of the Higgs boson particle in the summer of 2012. For the nonphysicists among us, the discovery was important because scientists had long wondered how the electrons, protons, and neutrons inside atoms acquire mass. Without mass, particles wouldn't hold together, and matter couldn't exist.

British physicist Peter Higgs theorized back in the 1960s that a yet-to-be-discovered particle must be creating a "sticky" field that helps hold the particles together. The discovery of a previously unknown boson in July 2012, confirmed (and named a Higgs boson in March 2013) would seem to confirm his theory.

Could you make this discovery relevant to nonphysicists? Well, you could begin by saying the discovery of the Higgs boson particle helps explain the existence and diversity of life in the universe. But the moment you got into the details about why that was true, people's eyes would probably glaze over.

Fortunately, most of the relevance problems we face are not that hard... although they may seem so on the surface.

Take, for example, this challenge: you want to make a run-of-the-mill charcoal grill relevant to a sixty-three-year-old woman who lives by herself in the middle of the Big City. And, oh yes. She is a vegetarian.

How would you make the grill relevant? Well, the first thing you would do is communicate that grills can do more than just cook meat—they can improve the taste of both veggie burgers and vegetables. So you might add a tag line to advertisements that would appear in vegetarian publications, like "Not just for carnivores anymore."

Second, you would move beyond the literal; you'd expand the idea that a grill is something that we use just to cook. When we entertain, invariably people end up in the kitchen. Well, an outdoor grill is like your outdoor kitchen. So, you can connect to the woman by saying her new grill is going to be the focal point of her outdoor entertaining.

Third, you play up her sense of independence. Traditionally, grilling has been the domain of men. You could position the grill as a way of her asserting that grilling is the purview of women too. (We are going to be talking more about these psychological factors in chapter 3.)

Fourth, you can market the grill as a way for your target customer to show off her iconoclastic streak. Grills are associated with people who live in the suburbs. Here is an urban woman—and a vegetarian, at that—who is using it (hopefully on a regular basis).

The point here is that segmentation is truly the answer to figuring out what is going to be relevant to your customers. But the definition of segmentation goes beyond the usual factors that come to mind, and it can also change radically due to circumstances or time.

You know the usual factors. You can segment your target based on: age, income, gender, education, geography, life experience, interests, politics, and religion.

And that is a good start. But you need to do more.

You can, for example, segment by situation. For example,

the Great Recession, which lingered from 2008 on, made certain things—including dollar stores, public housing, and ninety-nine-cent specials at fast-food restaurants—relevant to a large group of people for whom they'd never been relevant before because of unemployment and bad luck. On a more pleasant note, there is a reason it is extremely difficult to get a bad meal in either Paris or San Francisco. The situation in those cities—where the residents are highly knowledgeable and demanding about quality food—is such that restaurants that fail to measure up go out of business extremely quickly.

You can also segment generationally. Car companies were famous for doing this. Baby boomers will remember the old Pontiac ad that told people contemplating buying a car to "ask an expert." The experts in question were the young men—teenagers, in many cases—who bought Pontiac's muscle cars. And most of us can probably remember the "It's not your father's Oldsmobile" campaign, in which the offspring of William Shatner, Ringo Starr, Peter Graves, and Mel Blanc (Melanie, Lee, Amanda, and Noel, respectively) upstaged their more famous fathers and touted the virtues of the new Oldsmobile in the process. You don't even need to segment by a full generation. Australian-based retailer Gilly Hicks's target market is girls between the ages of about eleven and sixteen.

We will be talking about segmenting on the basis of thinking, sensory appeal, community, and values, as well as content, context, and contact in the next two chapters.

A FEW THINGS TO KEEP IN MIND

Obviously, once you segment you are *not* done forever. All the factors change quickly. For example, things that are not relevant suddenly can become so—and, of course, the converse is also true. Let's take an example of each.

Remember Apple's Newton? You probably don't. In 1992 Apple unveiled this personal digital assistant (PDA), a communication device about the size of a VHS tape, which had many of the features we now have in our cell phones (note taking, calendar, address book; it also had a primitive application that, like Apple's Siri, let you enter commands simply by saying them). The problem? The market was not yet ready for it.

As for products or ideas that have stayed too long at the fair, you don't have to look further than the back of your closet for the clothes you no longer wear.

> If you are not looking at the factors that make you relevant every six months, you run the risk of becoming irrelevant—very quickly.

As you go about segmenting, you can either start with your product—that is, you can think about how you are going to make your grill relevant to particular parts of the market, such as older female vegetarians—or you can start with what is going on in the marketplace and see where you fit in. ("Hmmm. People in their twenties and early thirties are the most socially aware, socially intertwined generation that has ever lived. Where do we fit in with that? Where *could* we fit in with that?")

Staying with the charcoal grilling example, Kingsford created a huge marketing campaign that encouraged friends and family to tailgate in their own backyards during football season. It was a big hit.

But it really doesn't matter where you start. The important thing is that you do. If you segment, you can connect more easily, and the connection can be made more deeply. You are truly solving a problem or making someone's life better. The connection has an emotional component, and that is what you are always aiming for. The emotional connection is what gets people to change behavior and/or stick with you for a long time.

If you don't segment, you don't connect. You waste your marketing dollars—it is much harder to get people to pay attention to your message if you are not relevant—and you will find it virtually impossible to grow. You won't be able to innovate—how can you give customers the new products and services that they require and desire if you don't know what their needs are? And you also run the very real possibility of never being top of mind again.

DON'T OVERREACH

Given everything that we just talked about, you may be tempted to move quickly (which is good), but if you move *too* fast, you are likely to make two extremely common mistakes.

First, you may make assumptions that may or may not be true in the aggregate, but are not true overall. For example, you could conclude, based on some preliminary research, that all Mercedes-Benz owners drink Starbucks coffee. There is a danger in making those kinds of overly broad assumptions.[1]

The second problem with moving too quickly takes us full circle. You could find five or six ways of making your offering relevant to your target audience and think, "Let's point out all six things to make sure we can truly connect." If you take that route, you run the very real risk of confusing people.

TiVo is one of Mike Maddock's favorite examples of this. He has convinced us that one reason it took so long for TiVo to catch on—and why it's now seen as just another form of digital video recorder (DVR)—is that the company was never clear about the need it was meeting.

The challenge for TiVo, like that for many other innovative products and services, is that it is capable of meeting too many different kinds of needs. It can record whatever show you want, so it replaces your VCR (you remember the VCR, right?). It can anticipate and find shows that you may be interested in watching, so it is a substitute for your best friend's recommendations. It allows you to skip over commercials, so it gives you more time to do the things you love to do. These are just a few of the many, many benefits of owning a TiVo, and they all sound great—too great, as it turns out. For the longest time, the company tried to promote *all* its features—presumably to appeal to as many people as possible—and wound up confusing the masses.

By the time TiVo discovered that perhaps its strongest selling feature was that it was easier to use than a VCR, it had squandered tremendous momentum. If its marketers had focused on a single insight/need and let reviewers and consumers discover all of the other benefits on their own, TiVo— a great product—would likely have dominated the market.

The takeaway: seize on the one or two things that are truly important to your audience, instead of everything that might be.

TAKEAWAYS FROM CHAPTER 3

1. **To make sure you are relevant, start by finding ways your product, service, idea, or candidate can make someone's life better.**
2. **Focus on the single most important attribute your product/message has,** because you cannot be all things to all people.
3. **When it comes to finding your audience, identify your core constituents** and move outward from there.

THINGS TO DO MONDAY MORNING

✓ Determine all the possible ways your product/service idea could be relevant.

✓ Rank them by the biggest potential problem they solve.

✓ Take that need and segment it, to get even closer to your customers and potential customers.

Try this exercise to hammer home what we just discussed:

As many times as we say they shouldn't, people still have a tendency to start with the "big idea" when they begin looking for ways to attract customers.

To prove why this should *not* be your starting point, do the following. Take five minutes and list as many revolutionary ideas as you can, even if they are not feasible. Include that perpetual motion machine, automatic desalination plant, and the like.

Next, try to find five business or consumer needs. You'll see it is far harder to generate the second list than the first. Even though creating the needs list is more difficult, that is the place to begin.

4

Dimensions of Relevance(II): Qualitative

Exploring the Relevance Egg

In chapter 3 we dealt with sorting people into categories based on the *needs* they have, in order to find ways to position the things we have to offer—our products, services, and/or ideas—in a way that is relevant to them. Here, we are going to talk about segmenting in an additional and different way: by understanding the *relationship* that people have with what we have to sell.

Why segment this way as well? There are a couple of reasons. First, the relationship people have with ideas, actions, and things isn't binary and it isn't equal. You may like your bank. And you may like your kids. But it would be wrong to conclude, based on those two statements, that you like your bank as much as you do your kids.

Second, the people you are trying to reach don't relate to everything in the same way. Again, let's use you as the example. The charitable causes you choose to be involved with may have more meaning to you than the kind of car you drive. But for automobile enthusiasts, cars might be more important than just about anything else on earth.

For example, in our four-quadrant model, which we call the Relevance Egg, we found that when it comes to commercial entities, the functional appeal, or thinking, was clearly dominant. In a commercial transaction people want value: the best price, the shortest transaction time, superior quality for the money, etc. In short, the primary question they ask when it comes to deciding relevance is: Does this transaction meet my functional needs? (As Harvard Business School Professor Theodore Levitt wrote more than fifty years ago: "People don't want to buy a quarter-inch drill. They want to buy a quarter-inch hole.")

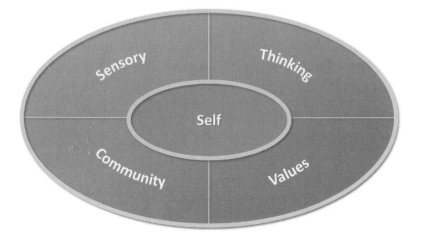

For "cause" or nonprofit entities, however, the functional element is much less important. When it comes to whether people will support a politician, political party or movement, or a nonprofit, what matters is values—what the candidate, party, or nonprofit believes and stands for and how well those beliefs and representations mesh with the individual's own convictions.

Third, not everyone who, on the surface, appears to be similar—men, for example—reacts identically to the same things. Generations tend to look at things differently, for instance. Men in their sixties living in an upper-middle-class suburb may resent all the money they have to pay in taxes to support their town's superior school system, since their children have grown and moved away. Men in their thirties and forties who have kids in those schools may not be crazy about their taxes, but they believe those high taxes are absolutely necessary for their kids' prospects of getting into a good college. That dichotomy makes intuitive sense, of course, but if all you did was look at how "men" as a group reacted to the question of local taxes, you might miss the point.

When it comes to people's lives, what is relevant changes dramatically depending on the category of product/service/idea we are discussing, and on the person's age, feelings, beliefs, background, history, etc. And that is why qualitative segmentation is so important when it comes to discovering what is—and is not—relevant about your offering.

Okay, this all makes sense, you say. But isn't qualitative segmentation incredibly "mushy"?

On one level we have to agree. But life is mushy, especially when people try to explain the choices they make.

Think back to our earlier brief discussion about how Americans are extremely compassionate. Well, compassion cuts across all four categories of our Relevance Egg in interesting and compelling ways.

- Empathetic actions can be practical ways of gaining favor with others.
- Compassion appeals to values of fairness and equity.
- Altruism is universally valued as a contribution to the common good of communities and clans.
- Finally, since emotions are inextricably linked, compassion engenders an emotional and sensory attachment that not only captures the imagination but creates a visceral connection with another.

Well-known and well-accepted behavioral research shows that we all make up "objective" reasons why we buy a certain kind of coffee or fund a specific charity, but such reasons rarely make up the entire picture. We often make decisions and then fit the evidence to support the decisions we have already made. That's just what people do. Someone can tell you that the reason he bought a Sony HD television is because he did extensive research or because "I had a long, positive history with the brand." All that may be true. But the real reason he bought the Sony? It could be that he liked the way the set looks when it is turned off, or that his friends are impressed that he bought a Sony

Bravia, or because he has fond memories of the Sony Walk-man he had when he was a kid—or some combination of all three.

If you simply asked this guy about the technical performance of the television—the quality of the picture and how little electricity it uses over the course of the year—he will tell you these were the objective, rational reasons he bought the set, but the reality turns out to be more complex. When you do qualitative research, you are working to identify the underlying reasons this customer chose the Sony. You are trying to understand the mushiness.

Once you have a handle on it—he gave you the two or three reasons he made the purchase that he did—you can begin some rigorous quantitative testing to see if what you found is right. What percentage of Sony customers are buying because the company has a superior brand name; how many are buying simply because of the way the set looks with the picture *off;* and so on. You can see what they say on Facebook. And you can gain additional quantitative data by "following" these customers around on the Internet to see what they actually purchase. But the key thing is to get data beyond the strictly rational (i.e., "I bought the Sony Bravia because it had superior pixel density"). That rationale certainly could have been part of the purchasing decision. The Sony television set may have had a great picture and better sound than other brands. And/ or the person could have gotten it on sale at his favorite retailer. But common sense tells you rationality is rarely the only reason someone decides to engage with a product or service. You want to get all the data you possibly can, so you can gain an understanding of why someone does—or does not—find your offer relevant.

There are limits to what you can get from numbers. People are not numbers. We are complex and confusing. That's why you want to do qualitative testing along with the quantitative.

When people begin looking for connections to relevance, they usually start with the rational, which, of course, is fine. But you want to do more. There is a reason that the relevance model looks like an egg divided into four parts. (See Figure 4.1)

The reason? Every one of us responds to several different dimensions—we interact with people, ideas, actions, and things based on sensory appeal, community support, and values as well as rationality (what we call thinking, in the Relevance Egg). As we saw with the case of the Sony television, a choice isn't necessarily based on rationality alone. To use another example: a pro golfer wants his clubs to be well made, exact, and dependable. But he also needs them to be comfortable in his hands and even to "sound precise" when he hits the ball.

So, the framework of things considered relevant changes based on the situation. (We will explore this in detail in the next chapter, when we discuss relevance and circumstances, specifically content, context, and contact.)

We believe relevance is the new communications imperative. We live in an increasingly chaotic environment, with ever-shrinking attention spans and ever-rising consumer skepticism. In a multichannel world, where people have more and more choices, making connections is not only more difficult but more important.

Could there be more than the four qualitative components we've named? Sure. One of the components we debated endlessly as we went about creating our four-part "egg" model was whether to give "emotion" its own separate section. It is clearly a big, big element in making something relevant.

That said, "emotion" cuts a wide path, appearing in three of our four quadrants. Clearly, senses trigger emotion; so do community (you love your family) and values (as the world's staunchest Democrat, you aren't fond of most Republicans). We could have separated emotion instead of including it as a subset of something else. Similarly, habit might have gotten its own place, instead of being subsumed into thinking and sensory appeal. (You often form habits because of the sensory reward they engender. For example, you have a cup of coffee after completing your first demanding task of the day.) Economic relevance could have gotten its own category, instead of being part of thinking. Then there is temporal relevance. What is important to you when you are a teenager may have no relevance to you when you are sixty-two. Conversely, what is important to you once you retire—access to the best hospitals and doctors, perhaps—may not have any relevance to you in your thirties. So we could have made temporal relevance a separate part of our model.

And, of course, we could have sliced and diced the information totally differently, using psychologist Abraham Maslow's well-known hierarchy of needs—physiological (food, water), safety, love/belonging, and the like—or have taken the psychographical approach used by the VALS (values, attitudes, and lifestyles) system and created categories such as innovators, thinkers, experiencers, etc., and approached the qualitative data that way. But even if we had used one of these other methodologies as the basis for our Relevance Egg, we would have ended up with a similar breakdown.

What we were aiming for was a framework that would help us understand how people attach themselves to ideas, causes, actions, items, and so on. We are not trying to segment *people*. We're trying to understand and *segment the relationship that people have to things*—the things being ideas, experiences, purchases, and the like. It is a subtle but important difference.

The four segments we've identified cover a lot of ground. The model may evolve, morph, grow, or shrink according to the needs of its users. We are focusing on the categories that form the basis for relationships that people have with things outside themselves. If others want to add their own categories to our list we are all for it. (For a look at how we compiled the numbers within the "Relevance Egg" see the Appendix.)

The point here is that you should think of these categories as diagnostics. We are not saying these are the *only* four things that matter. But this is a simple and practical way to categorize and structure your understanding of the way relevance is achieved; once you understand the four quadrants, you can weave a lot of elements, like technology, through each and every one of them. (You could ask, "How does technology change the qualitative perception of community?," for example. The short answer is, "Greatly." The Internet and, more specifically, platforms such as Facebook, LinkedIn, and the like allow people who have never met face to face to create communities that span the globe. Knowing that, you can ask yourself: How do we create relevance for members who live everywhere from Alaska to Angola to Australia?)

With all this as background, let's look at the categories in a bit more detail.

Thinking. This is the category that covers most of what goes on in the "left" (or logical) part of your brain. It is functional. It's concerned with the specifications of the product, such as where you can find it, price, and features. Most appeals for relevance start with thinking. "I buy it because it is cheap." "I chose it because it works." "I decided on this one because it fills an immediate and very functional need." This is the segment that includes all the rational appeals to people: "You need a car that is inexpensive to buy, and inexpensive to maintain? Have we got the automobile for you."

Community. Here we're talking about relationships and contextual elements. It includes such things as groups (broadly defined to include not only work groups—the National Society of High Tech HR Managers—but social groups as well—the Chess Playing Birders of Central Iowa), peers, social norms, professional norms (you wouldn't expect to find your accountant in a tee shirt, torn shorts, and flip-flops when you met with him to review your taxes), societal trends (when was the last time you saw a man over the age of thirty wearing a hat—not a baseball cap, but a real, honest-to-goodness derby, bowler, or fedora—without trying to be ironic), and cultural context (know anyone who is proud of being a smoker?).

Values. These are the ethical, moral, and faith-based elements that connect you with things outside yourself. This may include your place of worship, the way you see the world (whether you believe people are basically good or evil, and whether they deserve the lives they get or have their lives determined by factors outside their control). It can be as simple as a statement of what you believe—"I am pro-choice"; "I am pro-life"—to as complex as the way you view humankind's destiny. As this last statement shows, the values category can be extremely far ranging. For example, when it came to values, Ford scored higher than any other car company, when Brodeur partners surveyed people. Was it because the company didn't take bailout money when all the car makers were struggling at the end of the last decade?

Sensory appeal. The retail and hospitality folks get this one. This category includes everything you see, touch, smell, and hear as part of an interaction. That new car smell is the classic example of effective sensory appeal. The soundtrack that is playing when you enter a trendy clothing store is part of it as well. Sensory appeal also includes such things as comfort, safety, and routine. As we will see, this is an extremely underestimated category.

The Relevance Egg offers a way to see the many different elements that play into the concept. For example, retail brands have distinctive profiles. Most are organized around one or two characteristic elements. For Walmart, it is the practical and functional. For Target, it is that plus the ability to appeal to the senses, which may explain why Target has, by some indicators, outperformed its much larger rival Walmart in recent years.

You can dissect the information in any number of different ways and take the findings and look forward. And that is exactly what we are going to do in the next chapter.

TAKEAWAYS FROM CHAPTER 4

1. **Don't overlook creating emotional connections to your offering.** None of us is as rational as we think, and that includes our customers.
2. **Look to the four quadrants of the Relevance Egg to find places where you can forge that connection.**
3. **Don't worry about this model being "mushy."** People are mushy.

THINGS TO DO MONDAY MORNING

✓ Sort your products/services/ideas into the four quadrants.

✓ Create a list of your top customers and prospects.

✓ Look for ways to match those customers/prospects to the one quadrant where you think your offering will best resonate.

Try this exercise to hammer home what we just discussed:

The four quadrants will apply to every offering you have, even if it does not appear so on its face. With that in mind, increase your comfort level with the four quadrants by taking something that would appear to fit only in one quadrant and extending it to all four.

For example, how would you take the logical (thinking) Mr. Spock and make him appeal to someone based on the sensory appeal, community, and values categories?

How could you take a number two pencil, which we like because of its familiar feel, and make it appealing in the thinking, community, and values categories?

Can you take the League of Women Voters and extend its reach based on thinking, senses, and values?

Is there a way to make the Golden Rule—a values-based statement if there ever was one—even more important based on the thinking, sensory appeal, and community categories?

5

Dimensions of Relevance (III): Circumstances

Content, Context, and Contact

By now, we have probably convinced you that becoming (and staying) relevant is more complicated than you thought. It is, of course. And it gets even more complex. For example, relevance depends on the circumstance, and we can break those circumstances down into three parts: content, context, and contact.

CONTENT

The content of a communication—the words and pictures on a web page, for example—is the primary vehicle for delivering relevance to an audience. And that web page example gives you a pretty good idea of what we are talking about: words, pictures, video, social media in all its forms, and conversations. They all make up content.

And that content includes word-of-mouth, of course. Having your best friend tell you that you have to see the latest date movie is one hundred times more effective than any ad, trailer, or interview with the movie's star telling you how great the film is.

Because this social aspect of content is so important, we commissioned a study of Conversational Relevance, when it came to hotels, as a pilot project decided to look at the things that drive conversation and choice of hotels.

Not surprisingly, our research focused on the four quadrants of our egg:

1. Thinking (functional): The practical attributes people said they looked for.
2. Sensory appeal: What the hotels offered that was most interesting and appealed to guests' senses.
3. Community: Attributes of the hotels that guests were proud of and wanted to share.
4. Values: What they admired, the things that reflected their personal beliefs.

We looked at ten hotel chains: Best Western, Four Seasons, Hilton, Holiday Inn, Hyatt, Marriott, Radisson, Ritz-Carlton, Sheraton, and Wyndham. Here's what we found: Hilton, Marriott, and Four Seasons had the highest Conversational Relevance; these were the chains that people said the most net positive things about in social media conversations.

The key elements for functional relevance (thinking) were hotel service, location, and recreation; functionality of the room; and the rewards program. Marriott and Hilton got the top scores.

Key elements for sensory relevance were matters of sight (the view), taste (food), and feel (shower). Ritz-Carlton was the clear winner in this category.

Key elements for social relevance (the community part of the egg) were peer reviews, being considered "best in class," and being associated with something "luxurious." The Four Seasons was the winner in this category.

Key elements for values relevance were management and staff-based sense of service, luxury, and commitment to quality. Four Seasons scored the highest in this category.

But conversation, obviously, goes beyond what people are saying online or are tweeting. Say you are attending a party for the local hospital. This is not the sort of thing you normally go to. You are not a physician and your involvement with health-care professionals is usually limited to seeing them when you are ill or during your annual checkup.

However, there you are at the gathering, and the talk turns to the work some of the doctors' friends—physicians all—are doing in Central America. Normally, if you read a newspaper account or saw a TV clip about the work, you wouldn't give it much thought. Maybe you would make a contribution—you like the work Doctors Without Borders and International Medical Corps does—but maybe you wouldn't. (There are a lot of worthy charities out there.)

But this time you aren't detached from the discussion— you aren't watching it on TV or reading about it in a magazine. You are part of it, and you find the conversation intriguing and the good work the doctors are doing compelling and the next thing you know you are taking out your calendar and agreeing to spend one of your vacation weeks down in Central America volunteering. The fact that the content was shared in a personal conversation gave it a great deal more impact than it otherwise would have had. The circumstances made all the difference.

Let's dig a little deeper.

Content is more complex than you first might think. In addition to the usual suspects like conversations, commercials and media of all sorts, it includes e-mails—especially those that are "pushed" out by advertisers—and also the various customer relationship management (CRM) databases, which are mined for key words that might trigger a response in the target audience.

Say, for example, you are promoting something like an environmental group, maybe one devoted to preserving as much open space as possible. You would want to create content aimed at people who have a connection to the land. They might live at the beach or in the mountains, or someplace where they are surrounded by plenty of open space. In your communication with them, you would show the ocean, for example, but also people's interaction with it (surfing, boating, fishing). And you would stress how their contributions—be they in cash or in donated land—would help protect nature not only for people today but for future generations.And if you included pictures of kids—kids who could be the children and grandchildren of your donors—as part of those communications, it couldn't hurt.

This raises an important—if overlooked—point. In creating content, you need to keep the end user in mind. How could it be otherwise, you ask? Well, the answer is simple. Too often, messages are created by people whose primary focus is making sure the boss is happy with the result. The end user comes a distant second. As a result, the messages are crafted with the boss in mind. And what is appealing to a fifty-five-year-old male executive may simply not resonate with the target audience of thirty-year-old women. Or, to go back to the environmental nonprofit, it is lovely that the person who approves the copy is an avid windsurfer and parasailer. But those are probably not the primary interests of your donor base.

MORE THAN WORDS

Content goes further than the words we use—big or small, politically neutral or politically charged—to include the overall message conveyed. For example, for the longest time, you would find absolutely no hint of humor in an ad from a financial services company, brokerage firm, or bank. The thinking was, "You are talking about my money, gosh darn it, and there is not a single thing funny about the handling of my investments."

Well, you still aren't going to find many stand-up comedians stealing material from the ads of these companies. And the messages from firms created to serve the wealthy remain extremely serious. But some formerly very serious banks are now willing to introduce a bit of humor. See the ads Regis Philbin and Kelly Ripa appear in for TD Bank, for example. And there really is an institution called Redneck Bank. It's the Internet banking division of Bank of the Wichitas, a well-respected "country" bank established in 1913, which is "insured by the FDIC, like all legitimate banks!" Some sample copy: "We enjoy a good laugh, but taking care of your banking needs is no laughing matter. Redneck Bank is here for you with experience and good old-fashioned service! You'll find bankin' is 'funner' when you can open an account online offering high interest, no minimum balance, no monthly maintenance fee and many other free services!"

The Redneck Bank example brings up an important point when it comes to content. You desperately need to avoid making assumptions. Sure, money is a serious subject. But there is a certain segment of the population that really doesn't consider it to be a matter of life or death. And if a bank can offer free checking and is, indeed, federally insured, and you are one of those people who believes that one bank is basically the same as any other, then what the heck. Why not go where banking is funner? Clearly, Redneck Bank is not for everyone, but isn't that the whole point of differentiation?

Speaking of banks, here is our favorite example of how easy it is to make a wrong assumption. It comes from the book *The Millionaire Next Door:* one bank, convinced that it could boost profits substantially, set out to identify potential customers with a net worth of at least $1 million. These millionaires received glossy invitations to a presentation at the bank's headquarters. When these potential customers showed up, they found tuxedo-clad musicians playing classical music; there were champagne and caviar in abundance. The overall tone, in a word? Posh.

The party was a total failure.

These well-off people left as quickly as they could, having barely had a sip of the sparkling wine or a bite of the roe. The problem? These millionaires were just regular folks—men and women who had made their money opening a chain of dry cleaners or running a profitable box-making plant. They didn't drink champagne, and certainly didn't eat caviar, on a regular basis. A $15 bottle of wine or some imported beer would have been more than fine.

That story serves as a natural transition to the next part of our discussion of circumstances.

CONTEXT

By *context* we mean time and space. What is relevant in one context—what you wear to a baseball game—may not be relevant in another—how you dress for a fund-raiser downtown. You want to frame or position your message—give it context—in a way that is not only consistent with what you have to say but that amplifies it. Speaking of fund-raisers, let's go back to that environmental charity we talked about. If you want to deliver your message to its members, what would be the best way to get your point across? Well, based on what we talked about in the first four chapters, you would figure out who, specifically, you are trying to reach. In this case, the prototypical large donor is a woman in her early sixties who lives "close to the earth," meaning that she has a house at the beach or in the mountains or both—and has at least one residence near a large city.

So, if you were targeting people on the North or South Shore of Massachusetts, for example, you might stage an event in downtown Boston. Maybe you would arrange a tasting menu by a celebrity chef or a tour of the larger gardens within the city. You would leave the biking event or "fun run" to a charity geared to a younger, more urban audience.

Context obviously frames how you experience the message. But not only can someone create the context for you—the charity holding the event, in the case of the environmental organization, or the advertiser trying to reach you through your favorite television show—but your experience can as well. For example, if you are the child of rapidly aging parents, ads for eldercare, nursing homes, estate planning, and the like suddenly take on extreme relevance to you. What is relevant to you also changes if you find yourself divorced, widowed, or suddenly the parent of a stepchild.

Life events of any particular moment can create relevance. There is situational relevance. If your true love needs to be in Europe for three months, the ability to communicate via Skype, something that you had never really spent any time thinking about, suddenly becomes important.

Bank of America tapped situational relevance perfectly in a promotion that it used to run for college students (college is a specific situation if ever there was one). If you opened an account while you were in school, you were given five "oops" cards to present at the bank when you did something financially silly, such as overdraw your account. You'd present the card, and any fee for your indiscretion would be waived.

> At the highest level, context is incredibly simple. Do you sponsor a wet tee shirt contest or the symphony?

When we were talking content, we cautioned you shouldn't make assumptions. Let us give you something else to think about when it comes to context.

It sounds obvious when we say it this way, but people are more than one thing. Just because you are an investment banker doesn't mean you can't be a serious fan of rock and roll. And aging rock and roll fans could also be golfers. It's more than possible that the sixty-two-year-old environmentally aware woman we talked about earlier might like nothing more than to go hunting on the weekends. (This pastime would not be inconsistent. She could be targeting animals that are getting the balance of nature out of whack.)

All this argues for some interesting—and initially

counterintuitive—ways of becoming relevant. For example: Could you sell golf clubs at a rock concert? Not only are some of the concertgoers golf fans, but some rock performers (like Alice Cooper, Stephen Stills, and even Bob Dylan) take the game seriously and are surprisingly good. Maybe Callaway or Titleist could sponsor the next Crosby, Stills, Nash & Young reunion tour.

Similarly, could you bring rockers in for an environmental event? Again, a natural fit. Performers as diverse as Brad Paisley and Carole King are environmentalists.

CONTACT

The final part of the circumstances that govern relevance is the contact itself; how do you actually reach out and touch someone (as AT&T used to say)? Since everything we are discussing is from the perspective of the people you are trying to reach, here we'll talk about the source of the information they are receiving. Is it a couple's attorney daughter giving them legal advice or is it a high-volume law firm with another annoying ad that is interrupting their favorite television show? Is it their physician telling them about something they need to do to stay healthy or a direct-mail piece from a medical device company they have never heard of?

There are five different channels—points of interaction—you can use to reach someone.

Family. This category is broader than you think. As a marketer, you can, of course, have your message relate to a member of someone's immediate family ("A diamond is forever"; "What would happen to your family tomorrow, if you died today?") But your message could also target what are now called workplace families—a close-knit group of professional colleagues—and it can extend even further. University professors, for example, could consider themselves part of the same "family" of academics. Gay men and women may feel a sort of kinship, and so may other people with something significant—or just significant to them—in common, say, the family of Great Dane owners.

Economic. Here, you are touching on your audience's financial lives. For example, the message could be about financial stability. Clearly, you will need to segment based on age—what is relevant to someone in her twenties is going to be substantially different than what is relevant to a person in her sixties—but economics is a vitally important issue.

Community. What committees are they a part of? What's their religious affiliation? What groups are they a member of? Answers to these types of questions define community.

Society. This is community written large. With community, we are dealing with issues that you, personally, can have some immediate impact upon. What will the school board budget be? Who should be on the town council? When we are talking about society, we are discussing big-picture stuff: How will the European markets affect international trade? What about the U.S. debt? How serious a threat is global warning?

Personal. From the perspective of a citizen living in the United States, democratic protests across the Middle East are most certainly societally relevant, and perhaps economically (oil prices) as well, but they might not be personal, unless you have a friend or family member living there. Decisions about which clothes to buy? These are personally relevant.

TAKEAWAYS FROM CHAPTER 5

1. **Relevance depends on circumstances:** The *content* you deliver, the *context* you provide, and the way you *contact* people.
2. **Content involves every part of your message, not only words; the way you contact someone is vitally important and, like context, is often overlooked.**
3. **Not only do you have to make sure your message is consistent in each category, you must also make sure that it is consistent across all three.**

THINGS TO DO MONDAY MORNING

✓ Check to see your message is consistent across all channels. If you took away one piece of your message, would people still understand what it is you have to offer?

✓ Think about the content, context, and method of contact for your message. What can you do to enhance each part of our message?

✓ Revise your message. How can you make your overall communication more personal?

Try this exercise to hammer home what we just discussed:

We talked in this chapter about ways an environmental organization might try to communicate with its members. See if you can solve this challenge for the group.

The organization has high name recognition and is well liked. The problem is that it finds fund-raising difficult, especially on the East Coast. The group has done extensive customer surveys and found that people on the East Coast really do like its mission, in the abstract. But since it is far easier to buy land in places that are not particularly populated—like the mountain states—the organization doesn't preserve very much land in the East. And because it doesn't, people in that region don't feel a particular affinity for the organization.

Using everything we just talked about in the chapter, what would you advise the organization to do?

6

Relevance: Why Are We Making This Effort?

The Very Real Payoff That Comes from Relevance

We can't say this enough: the ultimate goal of relevance is to change (or maintain) behavior.

We can talk all we want about how to use various marketing channels/techniques, and we can think about the most efficient social media strategies to employ to solve the communication challenges we face. But none of that really matters unless we can persuade someone to our point of view (to buy our product or service or to embrace our cause) or keep our customers/clients/supporters from switching to someone else (see sidebar "Changing Behavior Can Mean Staying the Same").

When all is said and done, you want to make a difference; you want to affect someone's behavior. It's not about how many press releases you get out, how clever your ads are, or the number of hits your website gets. It's about getting people to come over to your point of view (and stay there once they do).

Relevance is the way to do that.

The world has changed to our disadvantage. We cannot push our messages through a limited number of outlets, as we did when there were only three television networks and a relatively small number of places where people could shop. Now, consumers are the ones in control. They have an almost infinite number of ways to engage with whomever they choose. They pick us (if we are successful). We no longer have an easy way to select them.

By being relevant, we show respect for the people we are trying to reach. We show we understand what is important to them. That makes it easier to:

- Get their attention
- Encourage them to consider what we have to say or have for sale
- Get them to change their behavior (toward endorsing something that is important to us)

And to do all that means you have to change as your audience does.

**CHANGING BEHAVIOR CAN MEAN
STAYING THE SAME**

We tend to forget about our existing customers, and when we do, it is always to our detriment. Yes, of course, gaining customers and/or market share is inevitably

---

a goal of every marketing campaign and communications effort we undertake. But as you go about crafting those efforts, make sure you are paying attention—and, we would argue, a lot of attention—to the customers you already have.

There are two key reasons.

1. If you gain a customer through your marketing efforts but lose one you already had because you weren't paying enough attention to her, you end up with the same number of customers—but lower margins. It costs far more to gain a new customer than to keep an existing one. So, staying even—by adding one customer to offset every one who goes away—is actually causing you to lose ground (in the form of decreased profits).

2. Conversely, there are times when, by remaining in place, you actually gain ground. Let's use a straightforward example:

You are a luxury car manufacturer that has 14 percent of the overall $1 billion market for quality automobiles. Your sales: $140 million.

Let's say two additional competitors enter the field, increasing the size of the total market to $1.1 billion. If you can just keep your market share at 14 percent, your sales will climb to $154 million; even better, since your share has remained the same, it means some

(Continued)

81

of your competitors will have lost ground to the new entrants.

The point here is simple, even if we tend to forget about it. A key part of relevance (and influencing behavior) is making sure you don't lose the customers/clients/members you already have.

Let's stay with the luxury car market example mentioned in the sidebar to illustrate how one company is keeping pace with its changing customers.

Loyal BMW drivers are not getting any younger—we are sure the car company would say those people are aging like fine wines, but their median age is climbing nonetheless—and so the company is going to great lengths to accommodate them and the aches and pains that can afflict an aging body when it sits still for too long.

For example, the new driver's seat on BMW's 5 Series is radically different—and far more accommodating than it ever was. "It is the most comfortable seat of *any* kind," said one brand-loyal customer. "It's like you are floating on a firm marshmallow. You are never going to have back pains from driving."

BMW changed as its customers did, in this case to accommodate an aging customer base. When it comes to your existing customers, you can never be complacent.

BUT DON'T CHANGE MAMA'S MEATLOAF RECIPE

You have to change as your customers' needs change, but let us stress the counterpoint to that. Don't change if your customers don't, and don't change if they don't want you to.

There are certain things your customers think are perfect as they are. And if your products fall into this category, change is only going to cause a huge backlash. Remember what happened when the Coca-Cola Company tinkered with the formula of Classic Coke? There were literally protests in the street.

Berger Cookies, based in Baltimore, understands this completely. If you visit the website—bergercookies.com— you will see that the company's packaging hasn't changed for decades, and neither has its recipes. Customers like these treats and their old-fashioned look exactly as they are.

When your customers love you, don't change. (You can add new products at the margins—line extensions for example—but leave the core alone.)

But why is changing behavior the ultimate goal of relevance? Couldn't the goal be to increase awareness or leverage other marketing efforts? It could, and no one is saying that improving what you are already doing is unimportant. Certainly, increasing awareness is worthwhile. If you don't have a voice in the marketplace, people can't hear what you have to say. So awareness is good. However, our goal here is to keep our proverbial eye on the proverbial prize. And the ultimate prize is getting people to change their behavior, and not something less like raising awareness or leveraging other marketing efforts you have underway.

Are we saying that your relevance effort is a failure if it does not change (or maintain) behavior?

Yes.

Is this going to be hard for some people to accept?

Yes, again.

What we are talking about is rethinking the way you do your marketing and communications efforts, and change is difficult—even in industries whose products are all about responding to or creating change.

Take biotech, for example. If ever there was an industry on the forefront of change, it is this one. It seems that every couple of months the industry comes up with a literally life-changing or lifesaving innovation. Yet when it comes to communication and marketing efforts, it is as if every single biotech company is stuck in the 1940s. They all do what they have always done. They hire lobbyists to help get regulatory approval; they employ a product-launch P.R. firm when they have a new drug or device to promote; and they make sure their investor-relations needs are covered. And that's it. Manufacturing firms take more risks.

And that is a key takeaway. A lot of marketing today has become an exercise in risk reduction. Firms are doing everything they can **not** to seize the future, but to keep something terrible from happening in it. That is no way to win the hearts and minds of the people you are trying to reach, and it is certainly no way to be relevant (unless you are a personal or corporate protection firm).

Fine, you say. But by making behavioral change the ultimate goal, aren't you putting more pressure on relevance than any of the four "Ps" of marketing—product, price, positioning, promotion?

At the risk of sounding like a politician: yes and no.

Let's start with the no. The four Ps describe the ecosystem we are working within. They are the four levers we can pull in an attempt to get someone to buy what we have to sell, be it a product, a service, or an idea. So, no, we are not trying to overthrow the cosmos. The four Ps were important yesterday. They are important today. They will be important tomorrow.

AT WHAT COST?

What is an acceptable price to pay for changing behavior? How much do you spend?

The answer is strictly up to you, if your efforts are on behalf of your company or your client. There is no hard-and-fast rule. Clearly, you want to be cost effective and you never want to spend more than you are going to get back over the long term.

That said, this is a decision that needs to be made on a case-by-case basis.

So, we are not going to stop paying attention to the 4Ps. But, and it's a huge but if you are doing the same thing everyone else is, you will never get ahead. At best, all you will do is tie them. And that is what is going to happen if you limit yourself to the four Ps.

By adding relevance to the mix, you are competing in a different, unexplored way. So while we couldn't expect a new kind of promotion to change the marketing universe—how many ways can you present "buy one get one free" (BOGO) differently?—we can and should put that burden on relevance.

> Marketing, when you boil everything down, is really pretty simple: you figure out who you want to sell to and then you determine the best way to get customers to buy.
> Relevance gives you an additional tool for teasing out both parts of that statement.

There is one last reason that we put all this "pressure" on relevance. As marketers, we get into a rut. We get good at our jobs and, once we do, we have a tendency to rely on the tools, approaches, and techniques that have made us a success. We get complacent and, as a result, we don't do our best work. When that happens, we do a disservice not only to our clients but to ourselves. Relevance, with its requirement that we change the behavior of the people we are trying to reach, can rejuvenate us by forcing us to come up with new solutions.

WHO IS AMERICA'S MOST RELEVANT RETAILER?

You can see the payoff that relevance provides as we set off to answer the question in the headline. Because we believe that relevance is the most important quality a brand, store, or experience can offer, we wanted to know who does it best.

We selected twenty-one of the largest retailers in the United States, including a variety of types—large discount stores, supermarkets, department stores, e-commerce retailers, and specialty stores. Using a technique called "maximum difference scaling," we compared and scored one retailer against another. That is, shoppers were asked to "test" each retailer at least four times against different combinations of competing retailers. Each time, they were asked to select the store they felt was the most and the least applicable in one of four areas that are part of our proprietary relevance model.

Practicality. We asked people in the survey to select the retailer they believe is the most dependable and provides them with the best value. (The "thinking" part of our relevance model.)

Values. We told respondents to choose the store they most admire, the one that reflects their personal beliefs.

Sensory appeal. We asked people to select the retailer that they find the most interesting and that most appeals to their senses.

Social appeal. We wanted to know which retailer participants are most proud to be associated with and offer

(Continued)

87

an experience they want to share. (The "community" part of our model.)

So which was America's most relevant retailer?

First place went to the retailer that shoppers click on but can't drive to: Amazon.com. Close behind was one that topped the list as the most interesting and most appealing to shoppers' senses: Target.

The one–two finish by Amazon and Target says a lot about what Americans look for and find meaningful in their shopping experiences. Amazon highlights the incredible power of e-commerce. It shows how technology can move a retailer from specialty online bookstore to a practical and value-driven superstore, one that surpasses even Walmart, the world's largest retailer.

The number two showing by Target underscores the importance of blending elements that appeal to shoppers' senses with value and dependability.

And what about Walmart? It finished a distant third. While it scored reasonably well in all four areas, the store's high ranking—it did finish third, after all—was dependent on its *practical* relevance to shoppers.

The good news? Our research has found that people view practical relevance as the most important attribute for a retailer to have.

The bad news? Our research also shows that the importance of "practical relevance" drops sharply among younger shoppers.

MANIPULATIVE?

And now to address the elephant in the room: How do we respond to a member of our target audience who says, "I understand that you are trying to change my behavior, but what I really understand is that you are trying to manipulate me."

The short answer is, we are. Not in a reprehensible way, to get you to do something against your will, but because we think you will benefit from the change. We are trying to get you to do something in your best interest—and ours.

(Continued)

We can't help it. When people talk about how relevance is manipulative, we always think of this 1970s cover from the humor magazine *National Lampoon*.

While we are arguing that you need to make your product, service, or idea relevant, no one is advocating holding a gun to your audience's head (or to that of their dog).

In offering you a product, service, or idea we believe in, we are making an honest case based on our understanding of who you are and what we sincerely believe will make your life better. It is up to you to decide whether what we have fits your needs.

Let's take a simple example. Were we trying to manipulate the behavior of teens when we set out to make smoking "not cool"? Absolutely. They, and society in general, will be better off if they never start smoking. So, the teens benefited from our efforts and so did our client, the Legacy Foundation. Nothing reprehensible going on there.

Okay, you concede, that one is pretty clear cut, and it is hard to argue against kids not getting cancer (and other smoking-related diseases, which costs the health-care system billions each year and leads to five million deaths a year worldwide, according to the U.S. Centers for Disease Control. http://www.cdc.gov/tobacco/data_statistics/fact_sheets/ fast_facts/).

But what about the situation where we are trying to get you to fund a not-for-profit? Doesn't our argument imply that we want you to donate to our client rather than to another worthy charity?

Not necessarily, although we understand the question. You could, of course, write checks to both organizations, but we concede that at some point, no matter how rich you are, you will run out of money if you try to fund every cause that is worthy of your support.

That's why the concept of relevance is so important. Yes, most of the charities out there are worthy of your time, attention, and funds. Because they are the reason we suggest you decide which nonprofits to become involved with based on a personal connection. Your kids are healthy and you feel blessed? Write a check to the local children's hospital. A loved one died of a disease that researchers believe is curable? Donate, so in the future someone won't have to suffer the loss you did.

Okay, that, too, makes sense, you say. But Audi over Lexus? Coke over Pepsi? Really, what is the difference? Your marketing/relevance efforts are pure manipulation, right?

Well, no. For one thing, there are invariably clear points of differentiation between two similar brands. Coke and Pepsi do taste different. And Lexus owners, who like their luxury with no muss and no fuss, hate the thought that you have to read the manual to figure out how to put air in the tires of a new Audi. Conversely, Audi owners ask, why wouldn't you want the air pressure in your tires to be as precise as possible so that you can get the most responsive ride out of this high-performance machine?

But leaving aside the differences between products, when we advocate one product over another, it is just that, advocacy. We are stressing what we think you, as a potential user, will like about the product, based on who you are. It is up to you to decide.

TAKEAWAYS FROM CHAPTER 6

1. **The ultimate goal of creating relevance is to change and then maintain behavior.**
2. **The maintaining of behavior often gets less attention than it should,** and that is a huge mistake. It does you little good to convert customers only to see them leave the next day.
3. **If your relevance efforts aren't changing and maintaining behavior, they are a failure.** Period.

THINGS TO DO MONDAY MORNING

✓ Measure how effective your relevance efforts are.
✓ Measure how effective your relevance efforts are.
✓ Measure how effective your relevance efforts are.

Try this exercise to hammer home what we just discussed:

You don't need to look further than the next mirror to sensitize yourself to what we have been discussing. Think about the last resolution you made (New Year's or otherwise). If it failed, ask yourself why did it fail, i.e. why/when did the habit you were trying to form or quit stop being relevant to your life?

If your resolution worked, what made it work?

Either way, how can you apply those lessons to your marketing efforts?

7

How to Become (and Stay) Relevant

Without Changing Who and What You Are

Why are you adding relevance to your marketing and communications quiver? We would have thought the overwhelming answer to that question would be something along the lines of: "I realize I need to compete differently"; "I am looking for a new and better way to connect with my customers (and the people I would like to be my customers)"; or "I want to stand out in the marketplace." In other words, we were expecting the motivation to be a positive one.

And people get there. Eventually.

But their starting point is usually on the negative side of the spectrum: a retailer sees all the department stores that have gone out of business, or a cell phone manufacturer looks at how the company that dominated the industry five years ago is now considered passé by consumers, or an industrial giant wakes up one day and realizes it is virtually alone in producing manufactured goods in U.S.-based plants. These are the kind of observations that lead businesses to decide they need to become relevant. The benefits of drawing closer to their customers become apparent later. The immediate impetus is remaining a vital part of the conversation.

> You can use relevance as a quick way of checking to see whether a new concept is going to work. The second you have an idea you want to pursue, simply ask a representative sample of people whether what you are thinking of doing resonates with them.
>
> If it doesn't, rethink what you have.

Having decided to become relevant, how do you sell the idea to your team? After all, they are the ones who will have to make it a reality. The danger, of course, is that they may see relevance as a flavor-of-the-month initiative delivered from on high; in that case, there is a real chance that they could listen to what you have to say about relevance and react with a rolling of their eyes and a "this, too, shall pass" mind-set. That can be fatal. As you know, organizations have an amazing capacity for killing new ideas.

To ensure that doesn't happen, we suggest that you begin by underpromising and overdelivering. By now, you understand that relevance can be a very important tool, but you don't need to present it that way. In fact, we would argue that you shouldn't. Simply talk about it as an additional useful tactic, another approach that your people can employ, and let them discover for themselves how valuable it can be.

Selling the idea to clients is likely to be (if anything) harder. For one thing, they probably have never employed anything like this before and clients (like just about everyone else) are not only skeptical but averse to risk.

Then there is the matter of cost. Relevance research, because it requires so many one-on-one interviews to get at the qualitative factors, tends to be expensive. When you add its newness to the higher cost, you can expect a lot of pushback when you advocate that a company adopt relevance as a marketing and communication tool.

How do you counter the probable negativity? First, by putting what you are advocating in context; then, by showing results.

Let's deal with context first. There are three points you can make:

1. **You are trying to gain a new form of competitive advantage**. Relevance is not just another variation on marketing's four Ps. You are going where your competition hasn't. And smart companies always want to gain an edge over their competition.

2. **You will be leveraging your market research.** Consider a company that is selling a new kind of electric saw to carpenters. The makers of hand tools are already asking craftsmen about sharpness, reliability, ease of use, and the like. But with relevance research you get at why the carpenter says, "I just don't like it," by asking about the way it feels and about how

quickly the hand becomes fatigued when holding the saw and even about the sound it makes.

3. **You can create greater ties to social media.** There is absolutely no doubt that social media is where an increasing percentage of your marketing budget is going to be spent in coming years, and relevance fits in perfectly. The quantitative steps that are part of the process—see our discussion in chapter 3—fit perfectly with the analytics you are able to generate from your online marketing efforts. And the qualitative component of relevance (chapter 4) ties to the "social" in social media.

Still, it is going to be a difficult sell, and that brings us to showing the potential outcomes as a way of overcoming the doubts your client may have. Clearly, you are going to provide examples that show how relevance has proven effective in the past. But while case studies—especially if they come from the same industry your client competes in—are helpful, people always want to know how they can benefit directly.

One route to take? Suggest a pilot project. That does three things, all of them good.

- First, it gets you underway.
- Second, it is a relatively easy way to get around the problem of the high cost of doing comprehensive research. You start with a small bit of research instead.
- Finally, it offers a chance to demonstrate what relevance can do.

THE MORE DATA, THE BETTER

One simple way to increase your chances of becoming and staying relevant is to take a hard look at the data on the people you are trying to reach.

Unfortunately, we don't do that often enough, and instead we make assumptions based on things we "know" are true but turn out not to be. That's a problem. As Mark Twain wrote: "It ain't what you don't know that gets you into trouble. It's what you know for sure that just ain't so."

Think about how the average American feels. Much has been written about the cynical, disillusioned American. Consumer confidence is down. Trust in individuals and institutions is at historically low levels. The political and social discourse is acerbic, unforgiving, and, in many cases, downright cruel.

No wonder you might conclude that the American psyche is troubled.

But the data from a survey by Brodeur Partners shows it is not.

- Americans believe themselves to be both empathetic and happy. More than two-thirds (68 percent) described themselves as compassionate and well more than half (58 percent) said they were pleased with their lives.
- Exactly half of us described ourselves as optimistic.

(Continued)

99

> - In the aggregate, generation Xers were the most likely to embrace the combined labels of compassionate, happy, and optimistic.
>
> Odds are that these are not conclusions you would have reached without looking at the data.

IMPLEMENTATION

When it comes time to begin a relevance initiative, people are always tempted to focus on the consumer. Where can we forge a greater connection? What opportunities are we not taking advantage of in the marketplace?

And that is certainly where you are going to end up. But is it the place to start? In an ideal world, probably. But not many of us live in an ideal world.

The fact is, you can start anywhere. Since that is the case, you want to begin by tying relevance to existing corporate objectives, in order to have a better shot at selling the concept. Those corporate goals will probably include customer needs, but there may be other ones as well.

Let's look at an example to see how this could work. Suppose your client is a supplier to the automotive industry and she tells you that there are three major corporate objectives to which every new initiative (such as relevance) needs to be tied:

Customers. The company wants to grow, of course, but its bigger concern is customer retention.

Competitors. The company is trying to gain the first-to-market advantage, so all new ideas should be just that, "new" to the industry.

Stock price. Senior management believes the company's shares are undervalued, and the executives are looking for ideas that will boost the price.

To show how relevance ties in perfectly with each of those corporate goals, you would address each in detail. For customers, it is relatively easy. You would, as we discussed before, do the qualitative and quantitative analysis to discover why people have been abandoning the client. Is it lack of product reliability? Do those products seem passé (i.e., no longer relevant)? Has another competitor come out with a better offering? Or is it something else entirely? In this case, becoming relevant could be a defensive strategy, a means to keep the customers the client already has.

Arguing that relevance can keep the company ahead of competitors is equally straightforward. Simply by using relevance, especially when the competition is not, the company gains the first-mover advantage that management seeks, and, presumably, the insights that come from it will lead to products and services that can keep the company ahead.

The argument for increasing the stock price is a bit harder to make, but only a little. What Wall Street is looking for is growth. Gail McGovern, David Court, John Quelch, and Blair Crawford put it this way in a *Harvard Business Review* article:

> The presumption of organic growth is baked into companies' stock value. If you decompose the stock prices of the leading consumer product companies, you'll see that future growth accounts for as much as 54% of the stocks' total value.

So what causes the share price to increase is a wildly innovative service or a hot original product. Think about what happens to Apple's shares every time it announces something radically new (can you say iPod and iPhone?). Is it any wonder that Wall Street believes innovation is the leading indicator of future growth and profitability? Relevance ties into that perfectly.

DO TRY THIS AT HOME

How might we apply everything we've learned so far? Let's take three hypotheticals and see. Our assumptions here are twofold.

First, our suggested answer to each scenario is based on the fact that we have done the quantitative, qualitative, and circumstantial analysis that we discussed in chapters 3, 4, and 5.

And second, our answers will only pick the low-hanging fruit. In other words, in thinking about the three scenarios we have provided only the easiest solutions. We have left the more innovative ones to you.

With that by way of background, let's walk through the three hypothetical case studies, starting with one that features a product. Specifically, let's say we want to expand the market for a niche product, the Swiss Army knife.

Scenario 1: Expanding a Niche Product

The quantitative and qualitative findings are fascinating. Far fewer people were familiar with the Swiss Army knife than we expected—those who are aware skewed older—but the people who know about it, love it.

This suggests all kinds of possibilities...and opportunities.

It would seem fairly simple to build off the company's strong base. Perhaps you could create ads showing fathers introducing the all-purpose tool to their sons and ads with mothers showing it to their daughters.

As for the four quadrants of our Relevance Egg:

Sensory appeal. The question is, does the knife feel good in your hand? Absolutely. But perhaps it should be easier to get the blades to open. Or should they be hinged to fit more comfortably in the pocket of your jeans?

Community. Clearly, there are people who use Swiss Army knives all the time. Campers? Boaters? Do-it-yourselfers? Is there a way to better tie in to those groups?

Values. Is there a difference between a knife and a tool? Is the fact that it is a weapon a problem or an advantage?

103

Thinking. The rational has always been the company's sweet spot. It might be time for a marketing campaign that suggests "a million and one uses" for a Swiss Army knife; it could show people—perhaps with a disproportionate number of them being women and twenty-somethings—doing everything from using the knife to open a large package to employing it to fix a balky kitchen drawer or a pair of eyeglasses.

Scenario 2: Making a Service Relevant

Can you make the U.S. Postal Service relevant? More specifically, can you convince people that the troubled quasi-governmental unit is an important part of their life today when we increasingly communicate by e-mail—not regular mail which is now often referred to as snail mail—and a significant number of people pay their bills online?

The research shows what you are up against. Quantitatively, people are unhappy with the postal service's speed and reliability. Both have improved since the post office's nadir, but no one is likely to say it is equal to FedEx, UPS, DHL, and other private mail services.

Qualitatively, the situation is worse. People hate the long lines at the post office as well as the fact that the offices seem disorganized. Added to that is annoyance that simple things—like finding the phone number for your local branch—are often extremely difficult. (You have absolutely no problem reaching the nearest FedEx office.)

What do you do?

Perhaps the place to start is by reminding people that the postal service is still viable and should not be automatically dismissed when something important needs to be sent by mail. You could point out that the service is far less expensive than the competition, no small thing these days, when people are trying to save costs wherever they can. As for the four quadrants:

Sensory appeal. Currently, this is a problem. Post offices are often cramped, government-designed structures that are far from inviting. But could you go back to the post office's roots, making the offices quaint and/or putting them inside another store? You can find bank branches inside your local supermarket. Why not a post office? To it's credit, the post office is experimenting with the idea.

Community. This strikes us as an opportunity. The post office, especially in small towns and the suburbs, is a place where you often run into friends and neighbors. What can be done to capitalize on that fact?

Values. This category offers another opportunity. The U.S. Postal Service has been around longer than the United States of America has. (The USPS traces its roots to 1775 during the Second Continental Congress, where Benjamin Franklin was appointed the first Postmaster General.) There has to be a way to take advantage of that history.

Thinking. In a time when you send a message around the world in seconds, is there a case to be made for having a national postal service? We think there is, based on price—you can mail a first-class letter from Maine to San Diego for less than 50 cents. The rationale also includes convenience: there is a post office in every town and many people with limited mobility rely on the post office for affordable delivery of medications and other necessary products.

Scenario 3: Selling an Idea

We tried to come up with as challenging a situation as we could. Try this: it is your job to make the National Rifle Association (NRA) relevant to the people who live in downtown Boston.

We concede it is a huge challenge. The standard joke among the (relatively few) Republicans who live in Massachusetts is that the Republican lever doesn't work in local voting booths. And while we concede that there are Democrats who are members of the NRA (statistics are hard to come by), blue state residents are not the first people you think of when you hear "National Rifle Association."

So, how would you make the NRA relevant to people whose first, second, and third reaction is going to be, "There is not a chance in heck it can be relevant in my life"? Well, you write off those people right away. There is a certain percentage of people who will never find your product/service/idea relevant, so don't even bother to go after them.

How would you reach the others?

Sensory appeal. If you are a baby boomer (or older) you may remember shooting rifles at summer camp. (This activity is still taking place at some summer camps, fortunately with much more supervision than existed in decades past.) We can argue about whether letting ten-year-olds handle a gun is a good idea, but there is no doubt that a certain percentage of us found shooting to be fun back then. Could the NRA tie into that memory and also capitalize on it with future consumers as well? After all, the Boy Scouts today use NRA-certified instructors and range monitors.

Community. This could be divided into two parts. First, there are people who like to hunt, target shoot, and the like. And some of them live in cities like Boston, so there is a (small) natural constituency.

The second part cuts two ways. Clearly, people are worried about the safety of their neighborhoods in general and armed intruders/gangs in particular. Would they feel safer if they—or other members of the community—were armed?

Values. For much of our country's history, rifles and the like were seen as tools as much as weapons. We hunted for food, and we killed wildlife that threatened our herds. Could the NRA capitalize on that?

Thinking. The argument is straightforward. The Second Amendment to the U.S. Constitution says, "the right of the people to keep and bear arms shall not be infringed." So, people are going to continue to own weapons. The discussion needs to center on the best way to do that safely, and clearly the NRA could position itself to take a leading role.

TAKEAWAYS FROM CHAPTER 7

1. You need to make a conscious effort to become (and stay) relevant.
2. Everyone on your team needs to buy in to this commitment to relevance.
3. With the commitment established, you need to make relevance another arrow in your marketing quiver.

THINGS TO DO MONDAY MORNING

✓ Make the case (at all levels) for relevance within your organization.
✓ Determine your starting point for engaging with your clients when it comes to relevance. Begin with what is important to them.
✓ Practice relevance by coming up with different solutions to the three hypotheticals we presented in the chapter.

Try this exercise to hammer home what we just discussed:

Identify your top five clients/customers.

Then figure out how often you are touching base with them.

Now, determine how often you *should* be in touch. (The answer is almost always "more often than we are now.")

What new information or ideas can you offer them, to justify that increased contact?

8

Relevance and Innovation

Why They Are Hopelessly Intertwined

You can't read an annual report, quarterly earnings release, or new product announcement without seeing some senior executive talk about the importance of innovation. And we agree that it is vitally important. In a world where everyone has the same access to capital, resources—human and otherwise—and technology, the only thing that is truly going to provide competitive advantage is innovative products and services.

Need proof? Would you rather be Google or Bing? Wegmans supermarket or Albertsons? Doctors Without Borders or Yele Haiti, the hopelessly incompetent (and now defunct) charity for Haitian relief run by Wyclef Jean?

Innovation is obviously a huge, huge deal.

So we are amazed that more companies and organizations do not tie relevance *explicitly* to their innovation efforts, especially when it comes to communicating and marketing what they have come up with. It would seem to be the most natural thing in the world.

And it would also seem that things are finally changing.

At a recent TED conference—TED, as you may know, is a nonprofit devoted to "Ideas Worth Spreading"—relevance was at the forefront. The theme for the 2012 fall conference was "Redefining Relevance," and it focused on how to best adapt and innovate in response to challenges of political, economic, and environmental uncertainty. (Hmmm, that's exactly what we have been discussing throughout this book. It is always nice to get confirmation that you are on to something.)

> It doesn't matter how you go about innovating—whether you create new ideas yourself or acquire them. Relevance maps to each part of the innovation cycle.

We sincerely believe we are going to see more and more people, organizations, and corporations exploring the ties between relevance and innovation in the coming months and years. How could it be otherwise? Consider the various steps in the innovation process, beginning with where the process should start.

STEP 1: DETERMINING NEED

You don't want to create a solution for no known problem. That's why relevance is important at the very beginning of the innovation process, when you are trying to find an unmet need.

> Relevance is a discovery tool that helps you find the need in the marketplace and develop the product to fill it.

The Segway personal transport vehicle might be a real cool invention and the Iridium phone, which allows you to call anywhere in the world from anywhere in the world, may be a truly revolutionary product, yet neither really fills any glaring need at a price that was affordable for the people who needed it. They aren't relevant to enough people to justify the money it took to invent them.

RELEVANCE CREATES USES FOR YOUR OFFERING

Whether we are talking about baking soda serving as a refrigerator deodorant, the corporate software program Dropbox being used by high school students to communicate with their teachers, or (speaking of students) smartphones being used by those in college to write their required essays, there are new uses for your product or service to be discovered simply by watching what customers do with your offerings.

Invariably, customers will find uses you never thought of.

Watch what they do and capitalize on it.

You can see how pivotal relevance is at the initial stage of the innovation process. If the idea is not relevant to a wide enough audience, the innovation is simply not worth pursuing.

STEP 2: CREATING A PRODUCT THAT FILLS THE NEED

Intuitively, you can see the importance of relevance in this second step of the innovation process. If your target audience doesn't think the product or service you have created fills the need you have identified, you are going to be in trouble. And, equally importantly, if the product doesn't keep up with your audience's evolving needs, you are going to become irrelevant.

For the longest time, higher education filled the need of providing postsecondary education to people who wanted to succeed in the workplace. The system worked fine for centuries: after graduating from high school, a certain percentage of people went off to college, got their education in classrooms on college campuses, graduated, and went off to fill white-collar jobs.

Well, the system doesn't work so well any more. The cost of higher education is climbing out of reach for many people, and in an increasingly digital society, many are questioning the value of travelling to a specific place to receive an education. Clearly, online learning is a way around this problem, but college and universities are struggling to determine the best way to deliver education using this platform. They have a huge incentive to try. The current model is becoming increasing less relevant each semester.

STEP 3: CONNECTING THE NEED AND THE IDEA

Once you have created the product or service that you are certain fills the marketplace need you have discovered, you have to make sure people know about it. Simply telling them isn't sufficient. We are all constantly bombarded with messages, and it is very hard for a just-the-facts approach to break through.

Your message must resonate. It must be relevant.

That's why you need to seize on the one or two points that are most important to your audience, connecting with customers through one or more of the options in our relevance "egg" (thinking, sensory appeal, community, values). You have to narrow down the benefits you are stressing, because if everything about your product or service is vitally important, then nothing is. Ironically, overcommunicating can make you irrelevant; too much material quickly becomes annoying. Think about the e-mails and catalogs you receive from retailers you like. It's nice that they are reaching out to you. You only wish that it weren't so often.

WHO RESONATES BEST?

If your innovation effort is relevant, it will resonate with customers.

Is there proof? Yes.

We gave a representative sample of Americans a list of the three best-known technology companies—Apple, Google, and Microsoft—and asked them which was "most interesting." The results?

41 percent said Apple

31 percent named Google

14 percent said Microsoft

Given the way these companies are being received in the marketplace, those scores sound just about right to us.

How will you know if you are successful in forging the right connection? That's simple. Your target audience's behavior will have changed as a result. Yes, they will have bought your product or service; but they also use it, talk about it, and stick with it.

A CONSTANT CHECK

Asking "Is this going to resonate with our audience? Is what we are doing going to be perceived as relevant?"

at every point of the innovation cycle can keep you from going off track. Failing to ask those questions can be devastating.

Consider General Motors in the 1970s. Looking for ways to boost profits, the car company made countless small decisions to cut costs. Plastic was substituted for leather; smaller, cheaper cars were added to the Cadillac line; and cheaper metals were used for all of the company's car bodies. Individually, these steps may not have been fatal, but collectively they drove the company into a ditch.

Starbucks faced a similar fate, and Chairman Howard Schultz warned in a now famous memo that the brand was in danger of becoming a commodity, thanks to all the cost saving and "efficiency" measures that had been introduced.

Schultz wrote:

Over the past ten years, in order to achieve the growth, development, and scale necessary to go from less than 1,000 stores to 13,000 stores and beyond, we have had to make a series of decisions that, in retrospect, have lead [sic] to the watering down of the Starbucks experience, and, what some might call the commoditization of our brand.

Many of these decisions were probably right at the time, and on their own merit would not have

(Continued)

created the dilution of the experience; but in this case, the sum is much greater and, unfortunately, much more damaging than the individual pieces. For example, when we went to automatic espresso machines, we solved a major problem in terms of speed of service and efficiency. At the same time, we overlooked the fact that we would remove much of the romance and theatre that was in play with the use of the La Marzocca machines. This specific decision became even more damaging when the height of the machines, which are now in thousands of stores, blocked the visual sight line the customer previously had to watch the drink being made, and for the intimate experience with the barista.

This, coupled with the need for fresh roasted coffee in every North American city and every international market, moved us toward the decision and the need for flavor locked packaging. Again, the right decision at the right time, and once again I believe we overlooked the cause and the effect of flavor lock in our stores. We achieved fresh roasted bagged coffee, but at what cost? The loss of aroma—perhaps the most powerful non-verbal signal we had in our stores; the loss of our people scooping fresh coffee from the bins and grinding it fresh in front of the customer, and once again stripping the store of tradition and our heritage.

Then we moved to store design. Clearly we have had to streamline store design to gain efficiencies of scale and to make sure we had the ROI on sales to investment ratios that would satisfy the financial side of our business. However, one of the results has been stores that no longer have the soul of the past and reflect a chain of stores vs. the warm feeling of a neighborhood store. Some people even call our stores sterile, cookie cutter, no longer reflecting the passion our partners feel about our coffee. In fact, I am not sure people today even know we are roasting coffee. You certainly can't get the message from being in our stores.

As a result of losing its way, the company followed Schultz's suggestion that it return to its "core."

The GM and Starbucks stories show that relevance can serve as a constant check that ensures you stay on the correct path—and lets you know what can happen if you don't check.

STAYING ON TRACK

Even if you have used relevance to find a hole in the marketplace, create a product or service to fill that need, and communicate your creation, you still haven't taken the link between innovation and relevance as far as you possibly can.

You can use relevance as a final check before launch to make sure that the link between need, product, and communication is as strong as it can be. And then, once the product or service is in the marketplace, you need to work hard to ensure it remains relevant.

The takeaway from all this: if your innovation isn't relevant, it probably isn't an innovation that is going to sell.

TAKEAWAYS FROM CHAPTER 8

1. The biggest takeaway is also the simplest: **you need to build relevance into your innovation efforts.**
2. **A focus on relevance needs to be embedded into every step of the process:** in the beginning; throughout development (to ensure you stay on track); and at the end (to make sure you have created something that people want).
3. **Don't close off the unexpected.** Invariably, your customers will find new uses for your products and services. Take advantage of that fact.

THINGS TO DO MONDAY MORNING

✓ Think about the biggest need your customers—and your potential customers—have. Is that where you are starting your innovation efforts?
✓ Make sure your people are checking for relevance at every step of the innovation process.

✓ Right before you are ready to launch, do a "relevance double check" to make sure that you are not about to waste your client's time (and money).

Try this exercise to hammer home what we just discussed:

Involve your clients in your innovation process. Here's how it might work: when you are about halfway down the road to creating your next product or service, show what you have to a handful of clients and ask for their input.

Then, listen to them.

Odds are:

1. You will end up with a better product.
2. Your clients will be more likely to become buyers because they helped create it.

9

How to Become Irrelevant

You Don't Want to, but You Could Be Taking Steps to Make It Happen

We are trying to be funny with our chapter title, "How to Become Irrelevant," of course no one *wants* to become irrelevant.[1]

And yet, without working very hard, you can come up with a seemingly endless list of companies, products, services, or ideas that have achieved irrelevant status, some within a very short time.[2]

> "If you don't like change, you're going to like irrelevance even less."
> —Four-Star General Eric Shinseki

Organizations have an obligation to stay close to their customers, and yet we are constantly amazed by the number of companies and nonprofits that don't spend any appreciable part of their marketing or research budget doing that. They assume that if they don't hear anything negative about what they are doing, everything is fine. Even worse, they can become arrogant (given their past success); they think they know best, so there is no reason to pay attention to what the market is saying. That can be a very dangerous position to take.

Complacency can be fatal because, when it comes to your customers, you are constantly dealing with a very odd tension. On the one hand, people are creatures of habit. They like buying the same things over and over again, having discovered what works well for them. On the other hand, they are always looking for products and services that are new, different, and better.

Perhaps the best way of dealing with that tension is by checking constantly with your customers and engaging with them in all four quadrants of the Relevance Egg— thinking, sensory appeal, community, and values.

As we have seen, stopping at the "thinking" segment is not enough. Take a software program that your customers use every day. It could contain glitches that drive them nuts, but they may never tell you because they find navigating through your customer service phone tree too frustrating. (To us, the phrase "For customer service, please hold" is not only oxymoronic but one of the first signs you are headed down the road to irrelevance.)

Instead of stopping at thinking, you want to probe. What is it about your product that your customers like? What do they dislike? What is the sensory experience?

Is your product boring? Interesting? Fun to use? And no matter how they respond, are your customers talking about their reactions with others, engaging the community portion of the egg? (See our discussion of the highest-rated hotels in chapter 5.) And what about the values portion? Some Microsoft users will tell you that if there was a small, independent start-up that provided a similar product, they would abandon Microsoft Word and Outlook in a minute. They feel trapped using the Microsoft Office suite of products and would welcome an alternative.

Now that we spent some time sensitizing ourselves to the issue of irrelevance, let's take a deeper dive.

THINGS CHANGE

One of the ways to think about irrelevance is to draw a comparison with extinction. Species become extinct because they are not able to adapt to changes in their environment. It is no different with ideas, products, services, or movements. Think about the Arab Spring the (literally) revolutionary wave of demonstrations, protests, and civil wars in the Arab world that began in late 2010.

When the environment that allows something—like absolute monarchy—to flourish eventually changes (in this case access to the Internet, rising unemployment, and rising expectations), the idea needs to evolve, or it will lose force and can be overthrown.

IT HAPPENS EVERYWHERE

It is not just companies that can become irrelevant, ideas and movements can too. Consider the:

- Ku Klux Klan
- Temperance movement
- Black Panthers
- Students for a Democratic Society (SDS)

So, you have a decision to make as the market changes: What are you going to do about it? In some cases, the answer should be "very little."

It's your product/service/idea, and it needs to be consistent. If it is constantly evolving, people won't know what it stands for. You don't want to be like that neighborhood restaurant that radically overhauls its menu in response to every new food craze. Fusion last week. Foam this week. Eventually, people stop going there because they don't know what kind of food it will be serving. The moral: you need to be true to who you are.

Ironically, you can be too obsessed with responding to market feedback.

Does this mean you ignore the changes around you? No. Take Brooks Brothers, a company known for selling classic clothing. The chain could have remained frozen in time, hoping for one of the periodic revivals of 1950s and early 1960s style—à la the television program *Mad Men*—to increase its sales. Instead, while it has remained true to its core, it has added "trendy" accessories—boots, scarves, overnight bags—to complement its offerings. These new items are of the same quality the chain has always offered—so in that sense, they are natural additions—but they are far more fashionable.

The car industry provides another great example of staying true to a classic that works. Despite all the attention to the rollout of new models and new kinds of engines (hybrids, electrics), pickup trucks remain one of the best-selling categories year in and year out—as well as one of the most profitable. And the models don't change much. Sure, the mileage gets a bit better, and there seems to be a never-ending race to increase towing capacity. But the basic truck remains the basic truck.

You can see the problem with not knowing who you are, if you take a look at what happened to *Rolling Stone* magazine. Founded in San Francisco in 1967, the publication was the choice of a generation when it came to music and, increasingly, (liberal) politics. But as its core demographic—baby boomers—started to age, the magazine had a key decision to make. It could remain focused on music and liberal politics. That would have meant ceding a huge part of the baby boomer audience to other magazines. Or it could try to follow the baby boomers as they aged, a perfectly rational decision, as those counterculture types suddenly had a lot of money to spend.

The magazine chose a middle ground and was pummeled from both sides. It lost credibility as the definitive source on the music scene—as newer, hipper publications and websites came to own that space—and became a "one note" publication when it came to politics (left-wing causes, good; right-wing beliefs, bad), becoming marginalized there as well.

The *Rolling Stone* example leads us naturally to discuss two other traps. First, it is easy to look ridiculous trying to be relevant to a group that simply does not want you to be. Think of those women who try to dress like their daughters and those fathers who think they are using the latest lingo but are hopelessly out of date.

Second, in an attempt to remain relevant, you can change before your market is ready. To us, extremely popular television programs are almost always guilty of this. Producers and writers take the characters and story line in entirely new directions long before the audience gets bored.

These two examples bring us to our final point about irrelevance: it may be inevitable, but why hasten your own demise?

Been to a record store lately? Drop off any photos to be processed? Used a pay phone? Read an afternoon paper (or been able to find a local morning one if you live in a small or even mid-size city like New Orleans)? Bought a printed map? Placed a call from your hotel room through the hotel's phone system? Ordered a set of encyclopedias? Rented a movie from a stand-alone video store like Blockbuster? Used a travel agent to book a simple trip?

Probably not.

And the trend of entire industries, professions, products, and services disappearing is only accelerating. Desktop computers are endangered; so are land lines and manufactured (mobile) housing (because of the glut of foreclosures on traditional homes). Faxes are now as quaint as dial-up Internet connections and rotary phones. The list goes on and on and seems to grow longer by the day.

In fact, it's easier to list the tiny handful of professions and industries that will remain unchanged in the next twenty years than it is to write down the ones that will be altered radically.

In many cases, you cannot fight it. Economist Joseph Schumpeter was right: creative destruction—Schumpeter's description of the process by which new and better products render those that have come before them obsolete is a hallmark of capitalism. And there are other factors that are out of your control as well. A merger can take away the budget for your next big idea in a heartbeat. But there is no reason to hasten our own demise.

That's why you need to fight becoming irrelevant.

TAKEAWAYS FROM CHAPTER 9

1. **Not only is it extremely hard to become relevant, it is extremely difficult to remain so.**
2. **Conversely, it is incredibly easy to become irrelevant.** It can happen fairly quickly. Just think of the last "big thing" of five years ago. (We will bet you can't.)

3. **One way to stay relevant is to remain consistent with who and what you are** and only change around the edges.

THINGS TO DO MONDAY MORNING

If you want to become irrelevant:

- ✓ Ignore your customers' ideas, suggestions, and input.
- ✓ Think you know best.
- ✓ Assume the world will remain the same forever.

Try this exercise to hammer home what we just discussed:

If you want to have a (depressing) conversation in your office, have everyone spend exactly two minutes compiling a list of companies, brands, and products that no longer exist and then compare lists. (There probably won't be a lot of overlap.)

If this doesn't bring home the importance of staying relevant, nothing will.

10

How to Regain Relevance

It's Difficult but It Can Be Done

It may sound strange, but the first step in regaining relevance is understanding that you no longer are. It is amazing how long it takes some organizations to come to that conclusion. They will blame product quality, service issues, or even their employees before they finally come to understand that they are simply no longer relevant to their customers and the people they would like to become their customers.

On second thought, perhaps it is not surprising that it takes so long. After all, one of the reasons companies become irrelevant is that they stop paying sufficient attention to what is going on outside the walls of the organization. And if you are not studying the macro trends (big changes in the marketplace) and the micro ones (what is changing within your industry in general and your business in particular), perhaps it isn't shocking that people stop finding you relevant.

There are two primary reasons firms stop paying

attention. The first is—to be blunt—just dumb. Organizations and, more specifically, the people who run them, become arrogant. When you have a hot product—or a string of successes—it is easy to believe that you know best, and that there is no need to listen to anyone or anything other than your gut.

TO REGAIN RELEVANCE, TRY THIS

If you want to be a vital part of the conversation, think back to our discussion in chapter 1 about what people say about your offering when you are relevant.

Customers respond to a relevant product or service with phrases like:

- I associate this product [or service] with values that are important to me.
- It stands for the same things I do.
- Being associated with it makes me feel better about myself.
- I want people to know that I am associated with it.
- It helps me meet my needs.
- It makes my life easier.
- It is not for everyone, but it is for people like me.
- It inspires me.

You need people to be saying at least two of these things about your offering, if you are going to have a chance.

Flip Wilson, the hottest comedian on the planet in the early 1970s, once said, "You don't have to pay attention to the little people on the way up, if you have no intention of coming back down." The fact that only a tiny percentage of the population remembers (or has even heard of) Flip Wilson shows that this is not a good strategy in life. And it is certainly not a good one in business.

The other reason for not paying attention is more benign but no less devastating. People become too busy to communicate with their customers. It's not that they don't want to. It's just that they are overwhelmed at work; they get so caught up in short-term goals and all the things that they need to accomplish day to day that they never get around to it.

And the problem is compounded by technology. As we automate more and more interactions with our customers—"press two for this" or "please tell us how we did by hitting one, two, three, four, or five on your phone"—we get less and less actual feedback. (The automated choices only let people respond to the questions *we* ask, they don't give customers the chance to tell us what they want to.) And as a result, we grow more and more out of touch, even though that is not our intention.

QUIZ: ARE YOU BECOMING IRRELEVANT?

1. **Are you studying patterns of behavior among your customers and changing as a result of what you hear and observe?** For example, the smartest retailers

(Continued)

---

noticed early on that twenty-somethings love extended shopping and dining hours. That's why so many fast food restaurants don't close until 2 a.m. or later these days and why stores are staying open later during the Christmas shopping season than they were even ten years ago. If you are not constantly watching what is going on in the marketplace, it is remarkably easy to become irrelevant. (The fast food restaurants that are closing at ten are not getting those late-night sales.)

2. **Are you quick to dismiss what at first appear to be exceptions to the way that business has always been done?** If, for example, you are in the car rental, movie rental, or retail business, and you said that Zipcar, Netflix, and Amazon would never catch on. There is an almost perfect correlation between a closed mind and impending irrelevance.

3. **Do you really know best?** Henry Ford had a legitimate—though not-so-great—reason for saying you could have your Model T in any color you wanted, as long as you chose black. (As the story goes, black paint dried faster and he didn't want other colors slowing down the assembly line.) But if you are needlessly restricting the ways customers can interact with or buy from you, you run the risk of becoming irrelevant.

> **4. Are you paranoid?** You should be. The easiest way to guard against becoming irrelevant is to assume you could become so at any minute and guard against it constantly.

How do you begin to regain relevance?

After you acknowledge that you've lost it, you need to make sure you have an extremely firm handle on what is going on in the marketplace, so that you don't fall out of step again. You need to be constantly refreshing your market intelligence. In addition to what you are observing, you want to be talking to your customers about what they like and what they don't about your offerings. What are they telling you about what you need to eliminate, change, improve, or add to your line of business? If you ask, people will tell you (often in great detail).

This is not a one-time thing. And although you can do a comprehensive review every six months, we recommend instead that you scan the marketplace constantly and do a quick check-in at least once a month. That's how quickly things are changing. It is not hyperbolic to say that almost every business today is a fashion business. And fashions can change that fast. So you need to create systems that allow you to track what has changed not only year to year but month to month.

For example, at one time, the ability to provide social media communications and attendant strategies was a differentiator for marketing and communication firms. Today, it is assumed to be included; it's the price of entry in that field.

QUITTING TIME

We are probably more optimistic than most, so it is not surprising that we believe that just about every company that has lost relevance has a shot at finding it again. Most companies, but not all.

If you completely lose touch with the marketplace—say, you are convinced that black and white, non-cable-ready, low-def televisions are primed for a come-back— regaining relevance is simply not going to be possible.

Similarly, the situation is basically hopeless when you have been overtaken by technology. (Yes, there is still a market for manual typewriters. But it's not a very big one.)

In these situations, it is best to call it a day or go into another line of business.

But for everyone else, there is hope.

Let's stay on the point of remaining vigilant at staying close to your customer and anticipating their needs. Adding more and better features and/or services is especially vital for keeping your long-term clients happy. You have a tendency to take them for granted. And they can take you for granted. And then one day everything changes and the relationship is gone.

Although we rarely put ourselves in our clients' shoes, it is easy to see why they can suddenly conclude that you are no longer relevant for them and move on. Let's say Big Bank A has handled all of your company's financial needs for years. It is the end of the year, and they send you and your employees annual 401k statements. And then it hits you. You can't remember the last time you checked on what other options, services, and products are available to you when it comes to taking care of your financial needs. And so you start asking yourself: "Are we getting the best returns? Is Big Bank A offering us the best options? Are things as wonderful as they possibly can be?"

It was not that there was anything wrong with the relationship. It's just that you hadn't thought about it for a while, and now that you are, you have some questions about whether you're getting the best deal possible.

If you took your concerns to Big Bank A, it is very likely that the relationship would continue. The bank representative would tell you of other options that are available and might tweak what it was providing to you, if you pointed out that you could probably get a better deal elsewhere.

The pace of innovation is brisk, and your clients' desire to get the absolute most out of every dollar they spend is intense. That's why you need to constantly show you are adding value.

But you—like many of *your* customers—might feel uncomfortable asking about better terms or other options. It could strike you as being confrontational, and most people don't like making a scene, even if it is an extremely polite one. And so, you begin looking around and eventually you find another financial institution that is offering a better deal or is more in sync with your needs, and you end up moving your business there—all because Bank A let the relationship languish. The bank didn't do anything overtly wrong. But because it didn't actively manage the relationship—because it was not constantly checking that it was remaining relevant to you—it lost a customer.

SORT OF RELEVANT?

As the old saying goes, you can't be a little bit pregnant. You either are or you are not.

But you *can* be a little bit relevant, especially when it comes to geography. Consider the Kittery Trading Post, which, as the Maine retailer points out on its website, "has been outfitting people for the great outdoors since 1938."

It offers fishing and camping gear, water sports equipment, and its hunting and shooting section includes "everything you need to hunt game or practice marksmanship. From ammunition, magazines, and targets to hunting accessories such as scents, calls, decoys, and field dressings."

It's a wonderful store. But its relevance is limited by geography. Sure, people in rural Maine are great potential customers, but people in the big city? Not so much. For urban dwellers, Kittery Trading Post is irrelevant without ever having been relevant.

THE RATE OF CHANGE

We touched on this earlier, but let's go more in depth here about just how fast the world is changing.

In a TED talk (you can see it on YouTube[1]), Rick Warren, an evangelical Christian pastor and author who founded the Saddleback megachurch in Lake Forest, California, said that an organization becomes irrelevant when the speed of change outside of it is faster than the rate of change inside. And he is absolutely right. If you can't keep up with what is happening around you, you are destined to fall hopelessly behind.

This means that putting systems in place to capture changes in the marketplace is not enough. You need to make sure that your organization is keeping up with everything that is happening outside your walls. And you have to stay current on the inside as well as the outside.

You may not be able to do it on your own. We all would like to think we are able to keep up with what is going on both inside and outside our organizations, but we may not be objective judges of how well we are doing. You may want to turn to your board, a local university professor, or even trusted friends for their perspectives on your performance.

It is possible, of course, that you are watching for trends, have created this amazing relevance dashboard, and are an absolutely open-minded and impartial judge of how well you are doing in keeping up with changes in the marketplace. But if you are, you are the rare exception. Most of us could use some help. And, in fact, what we recommend is that you combine your best efforts with some assistance from the outside in judging your performance. Because even if you are very good at one part of our Relevance Egg, say, the thinking part, and understand on a logical basis why customers buy from you (or stay away), you may need help with the other three quadrants. You don't want to be one dimensional.

NUTS AND BOLTS

To correct your irrelevance problem, obviously you are going to attack from all angles. You are going to look at your:

- Product and service offerings
- Leadership style
- Corporate culture

As you do, let us give you three things to guard against. First, if you are going to ask people for their opinions, you'd better listen (and respond) to what they have to say. The worst thing you can do is ask someone what he thinks, have him go on at great and considered length, and then, when he is done, continue to do business as you were before he responded. If you ignore someone's comments, you are never going to get honest feedback from him again.

The second point is related to the first: you get the culture you deserve. Leaders must model the behavior that they want. If you are closed off to new ideas, you can bet your employees will be as well.

Third, if you are going to make a big deal out of your efforts to become relevant once again, make sure that you really are becoming so. Two examples from General Motors will make the point about what you should and should not do here.

Remember the "Not your father's Oldsmobile" campaign we talked about in chapter 3? It was the GM brand's way of saying that its cars—which were known for being big and offering a couch-like ride—had changed and now were sporty and relevant to a younger audience. Well, they weren't, and Oldsmobile failed on two levels.

The first? The company didn't attract younger buyers. These buyers took one look at the new cars and said, "Nope, it is still my dad's Oldsmobile."

Second, Oldsmobile alienated its traditional base. Who wants to buy a product from a company that says to them: "You are an old fuddy-duddy."

For the longest time, GM's not-so-secret marketing

strategy was to introduce young customers to the GM family of cars by getting them to buy the company's low-end products—like Chevrolet and Pontiac. The goal then was to get them to trade up to more expensive brands as they grew older and made more money. Someone who initially bought a Chevrolet Biscayne, the line's lowest-price offering, might move up to a Chevy Impala when he bought his second car, before moving on to a Buick or an Oldsmobile for his third.

The "Not your father's Oldsmobile" line killed off that marketing strategy forever. Why would an older customer aspire to buy something that was designed for his kids? This customer's trade-up car of choice became an Infiniti or an Acura, not an Oldsmobile. As a result, the Oldsmobile line died out. Conversely, GM's Cadillac brand had been all but written off. Yes, it had a loyal customer base of people in their late fifties and well into their sixties, but the problem was that those people don't buy all that many cars, and the generation coming up behind them had no interest in a car associated with their grandfathers.

TO THINE OWN SELF BE TRUE

As we have said throughout: you want to be relevant. But not at the cost of being something that you are not.

One reason the "Not your father's Oldsmobile" campaign failed was that the redesigned Oldsmobile never was a hip, sporty car, and pretending that it was just

---

seemed silly. In contrast, Cadillac was able to regain relevance by building off its core strengths of making powerful, well-built cars.

You never want to become relevant by guessing where the market is going and trying to get there first. You want to build off your strengths. As long as you know who you are, you can add to your brand's core assets.

Beginning with the introduction of the Escalade in the early 2000s, GM served notice that it was changing. It followed up with a new generation of cars and advertising, both of which were designed to give potential buyers who would previously have shunned the line a reason to take a second look. They did, and Cadillac has regained relevance.

TAKEAWAYS FROM CHAPTER 10

1. **The first step in regaining relevance is deciding you want to.**
2. **Regaining relevance is like starting over.** Re-create relevance in the same way you created it in the first place. Start with a core group of customers and build from there.
3. **In your attempt to win back market share, be careful not to overpromise.** If you disappoint a customer twice, she is gone forever.

THINGS TO DO MONDAY MORNING

✓ Create systems that will keep you from losing track of what is happening in the marketplace.
✓ Constantly monitor those systems.
✓ Go to the customers you have lost; apologize for disappointing them and point out in detail what you are going to do better in the future.

Try this exercise to hammer home what we just discussed:

Return to the basics. Go to the four quadrants of the Relevance Egg and take an objective look at why you lost your way. If you can't figure it out, or if you come to conclusions such as "It wasn't us, it was them," bring in some people from the outside to help you.

Once you figure out the problems, come up with multiple plans to correct them.

Final Takeaways

What We Have Learned

Let's end the way we began.

As we said back in chapter 1:

> Organizations like yours spend, in total, billions of dollars annually to get people to buy a product, embrace a brand, follow a candidate, or join a cause. And yet we can all agree these marketing campaigns, ads, public relations initiatives, communication programs, and social change efforts are—to be kind—often less effective than they could be.

One way we can increase our effectiveness is to become relevant, by being practically (and especially) socially applicable. As we have seen, both the practical and the social parts of the equation are necessary. You must fill a need, and there also has to be an emotional connection if you are going to create "stickiness," that is, if you want people to return to you time and time again.

If what you are offering isn't relevant, nothing else matters. Your strategy is ruined, and so are your tactics. You want people to respond to your marketing initiatives. They won't if there is no reason to, that is, if your products or services are not relevant.

How do you go about building those meaningful commitments? As we saw, there are three different ways: by segment, by the intagibles, and by circumstances.

By segment. You cannot be all things to all people. If you try, you end up diluting your message so much that you don't stand for anything. But you can be relevant to all people based on some things. You achieve that by dividing your marketing based on specific factors: age, income, gender, education, geography, life experience, interests, politics, or whatever. You then determine how you can make what you have relevant to people in each of those categories.

CAN YOU ALWAYS BE RELEVANT?

The answer to the question—can you always find a way to be relevant to someone—is "yes," with two caveats.

First, you can't make a terrible product or provide a lousy service. Things that fall apart or make our lives less appealing are never going to be relevant, no matter how hard you try.

Second, when you are dealing with the very technical (complex engineering) or extremely specialized (theoretical physics), you simply may not be able to forge the emotional resonance you seek beyond an extremely small number of people.

By the intangibles. These are the thinking, sensory appeal, community, and values parts of our Relevance Egg.

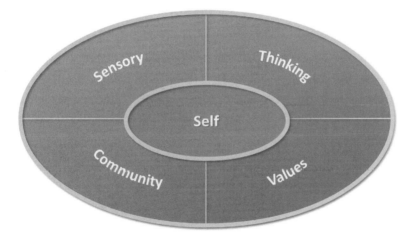

There are limits to what you can get from numbers. People are not numbers. We are a complex and confusing species. That's why you want to do qualitative testing along with the quantitative.

By circumstances. There's relevance of content (the words, pictures, and other elements of our communications), context (the time and space within which an interaction takes place), and contact (the communication's source and medium).

SIMPLE? YES. EASY? NO

The ultimate goal of relevance is to change (or maintain) behavior. We can talk until the cows come home about how to use various marketing channels/techniques and ask ourselves what are the most efficient social media strategies to solve the challenges we face. But none of that really matters unless we can persuade someone to our point of view (to buy our product/service or embrace our cause) or keep the customers/clients/supporters we have from switching to someone else. As you know, this isn't easy. And you will probably need some help, for four very specific reasons.

One, we all have a tendency to overrate how well we are doing. Think back to our discussion of Lake Wobegon in chapter 1—our tendency as humans is to assess ourselves generously.

Second, our customers are getting far more demanding. It wasn't that long ago that we could ask them to choose on the basis of excellent service or low cost. Today, if you ask customers, "Do you want terrific service or the absolutely lowest price," they always answer, "Both."

Third, it is extremely difficult—and it is getting harder all the time—to get through to people. They—like you— are extremely pressed for time. And they—again, like you—have an ever-growing distrust of the messages they receive. (When was the last time you took at face value a company's or product's claim that it was "the best" or "highest quality" or "cheapest"?)

And finally, we are all worried. We worry about our families, of course, but also about the economy and what is happening in the world. It may not actually be becoming a scarier place, but it sure seems that way.

So, becoming—and staying—relevant is a challenge. The payoff makes it worthwhile.

We wish you good luck.

Organizational Relevance: Frameworks and Profiles

A STUDY BY BRODEUR PARTNERS

(Note: This is an abridged version of our study. If you would like a full copy of the report, please send us an e-mail at Relevance@Brodeur.com).

What makes an organization relevant? Is it that the organization meets a personal need or performs a special function? Is it because it makes a particular product or provides a specific service; and because of those useful functions or products, do people find some organizations more relevant than others? Do they think of and connect to organizations in different ways? Does organizational relevance matter?

This is the first of several studies by Brodeur Partners exploring the dimensions of relevance. If you want to receive the subsequent ones (for free), just send us a note at: Relevance@Brodeur.com

Why relevance? We believe relevance is the new communications imperative. We live in an increasingly chaotic media environment with ever-shrinking attention spans and rising consumer skepticism. In a multichannel world, where people have more and more choices, making connections is not only more difficult, it is more important.

In this study, we set out to answer two simple questions: **First, does the framework of things that people consider relevant change based on the type of organization?** For instance, are the factors we find meaningful and relevant for a nonprofit the same as those we find relevant for a business? Are the things we find relevant for our favorite charity the same as those we find relevant for our favorite bank, car manufacturer, or retailer?

Second, do organizations and businesses have particular "relevance profiles"? Do some organizations connect to people through values, others through personal need, and others through curiosity and excitement? In other words, do organizations have "relevance profiles" that define the way people view and interact with them? And beyond the question of profiling, do the depth and breadth of connections, or "points of relevance," correlate to better organizational and business performance?

To find answers to these questions we conducted an online survey of 2,022 American consumers between the ages of eighteen and sixty-five. The survey was conducted by the independent opinion research firm The Prime Group LLC from February 15th through the 20th, 2012. Results were weighted to reflect the national population. What follows are the results of that study.

150

SUMMARY OF FINDINGS

• **What people find meaningful in nonprofit organizations is very different from what they find meaningful in commercial organizations.** By far the most relevant characteristics for a nonprofit are values-related. *Does that charity reflect my convictions?* The next most important thing is for the charity to inspire. For the types of commercial organizations we tested, the framework was much different. The most meaningful factors for those commercial organizations were meeting personal needs and, after that, values.

• **What people find meaningful in commercial organizations does not change, regardless of sector.** We asked people to consider professional services firms, high-end product companies, and consumer products companies. In all three cases, the profiles of what people thought most and least important were extremely similar.

• **Many companies appear to have specific leading relevance indicators.** Companies such as Apple, Target, and Red Bull are distinctively "interesting and exciting." Ford scores high on values. Google and Walmart are distinctive in their ubiquity and would be missed most if they were gone.

• **Several companies that were much smaller in size and scale appear to be more "relevant" to consumers than larger companies.** We found this among the automotive, retail, and telecommunications companies tested.

• **High relevance scores appeared to correlate with superior growth and performance, even though the companies with high relevance scores were much smaller than their competitors.** It is unclear whether high relevance leads to superior growth or whether superior growth and performance lead to greater relevance. In any case, there does appear to be a clear correlation.

• **The winner among government agencies was the department most often considered for elimination.** We asked people to consider five very different government agencies in the fields of defense, health, environment, finance, and education. The winner was education.

RELEVANCE FRAMEWORKS: OUR APPROACH

We asked people to evaluate eight different statements (each suggesting a distinct pathway to relevance) and select the statement they thought was the **most** and **least** meaningful for each type of organization. We split the sample of 2,000 into random cells of approximately 500 people and had each group evaluate one of the following types of organizations:

- *Charities and nonprofits,* organizations you might support through donations or volunteering, e.g., a church, a charity, or a political party.
- *Professional services,* companies that provide personal or professional services to you, e.g., your bank, a real estate agency, or a credit card company.

- **High-end goods retailers,** companies that sell durable products to you, such as automobiles, computers, or televisions.
- **Personal products retailers,** companies that sell personal items to you, such as clothing, jewelry, or sporting goods.

We used a survey instrument/method called *adaptive conjoint (or MaxDif)* to ensure that respondents evaluated each statement in context. On a series of five screens respondents saw four different relevance statements. On each screen, respondents were asked to choose the *most* and *least* meaningful statement for that type of organization. Statements would reappear several times, always in a different mix. The more often a relevance statement was selected as *most* meaningful, the higher its value score. The eight statements tested were:

- I associate it with values that are important to me.
- It stands for the same things I do.
- Being associated with it makes me feel better about myself.
- I want people to know that I am associated with it.
- It helps me meet my needs.
- It makes my life easier.
- It is not for everyone but it is for people like me.
- It inspires me.

RELEVANCE FRAMEWORKS: OUR FINDINGS

We found that the relevance statements people consider most and least meaningful for a nonprofit organization are very different from those they consider most and least meaningful for a commercial organization.

Of the eight relevance statements we tested, by far *the most important characteristics for a nonprofit were values-related.* In thinking about charities and nonprofits, people said the most meaningful thing was that they associate the organization "with values that are important to me."[1] A close second was that it "stands for the same things I do." Third was that the organization "inspires me."

By contrast, *among all three categories of commercial organizations tested, the most important characteristics were function- or need-related.* The most important factor was that a company "helped me meet my needs." A close second was that it "made my life easier." The two values statements—"values that are important to me" and "stands for the same things I do"—were third and fourth, respectively.

The study suggests that people's "relevance framework" for charities and nonprofits is profoundly different from the framework they have for businesses. For charities and nonprofits, the most important thing for consumers is that the organization has values that they can both admire and share. Beyond that, people want nonprofits to inspire.

The data suggests that nonprofits connect with followers in a very different way than companies do with customers. The personal connection to nonprofits is less about efficiency or efficacy and much more about demonstrating a shared mission. Moreover, the data suggest that nonprofits may not want to sacrifice programs that inspire and motivate—things often viewed as overhead—at the expense of being "efficient." Why? Because inspiration and motivation are at the heart of what makes a nonprofit relevant to its followers. In fact, inspirational activities could be a significant way in which a nonprofit both shows and shares its values with its supporters.

THE COMMERCIAL RELEVANCE PROFILE

Among the three categories of commercial organizations— personal products, high-end products, and professional services—there was an amazing consistency with regard to the relevance statements respondents found most meaningful.

The data suggest that, regardless of whether you are a bank, auto maker, or apparel company, the most important thing is to show that you are either meeting a "specific need" or making someone's life "easier." This functional or need-driven consideration appears to be a relevance threshold point for commercial relevance.

Beyond that, consumers are looking for companies that share their values. People chose the statement "I associate it with values that are important to me" as the third most important for all three commercial categories tested. Although small, there was a slight increase in the importance of values in the two categories that represented high-priced goods and services.[2] This could suggest that the relevance of "values" as a concept increases with potential cost and personal investment.

FUNCTION VERSUS VALUES

We looked at several different models based loosely on the Brodeur Partners four-quadrant approach based on the thinking, social (community), values, and sensory self.

Statement	Category
I associate it with values that are important to me	Values
It stands for the same things I do	
Being associated with it makes me feel better about myself	Social
I want people to know I'm associated with it	
It helps me meet my needs	Thinking
It makes my life easier	
It is not for everyone but it is for people like me	Aspirational
It inspires me	

We looked at the total commercial sample, did a simple analysis, and found that there were two dominant types of people: the functional or rationally driven and the values-driven. The rationally driven group represents approximately three-quarters of Americans (77 percent). The values-driven group represents about one in five Americans (18 percent). We then looked at some of the demographic data to see what makes for a values-based consumer and what makes for a functional-based consumer.

The results may surprise you. *While the two groups were very similar, the values-driven consumers tend to be more religious, more civically engaged, and more Republican. That is, the values-driven consumer appears to be more conservative.* This may seem to some to be counterintuitive in that many equate "values" with liberal causes. Not so, according to this data. "Values" could just as easily be equated with issues associated with conservative causes like sanctity of life, fiscal discipline, and personal responsibility.

RELEVANCE PROFILES: OUR APPROACH

The second part of the study examined whether people connected or related to specific companies and organizations differently. We looked at different sets of well-known brands in commercial and nonprofit sectors. The commercial groups included automotive, retail, technology communications, beverages, and athletics organizations. The nonprofit groups were health care, emergency services, environmental, and government.

We asked respondents to consider a set of companies and organizations, and in each category select the **one** organization that:

- Is closest to my own values
- Is most interesting and exciting
- I would miss most if it were gone
- I would most want to be publicly associated with it
- I would most want to do business with it

It is important to note that the following data is comparative. That is, people were asked to judge among a defined set of companies and organizations. As in any contest or election, the selections or "votes" could shift significantly if the choices were different.

In each category we tried to identify a manageable list of organizations (fewer than six) that represented a mix of large and small well-known brands, including the brand leaders in that category.

In our analysis we looked for differences or gaps between measures inside a company's ranking. That is, we looked at whether a company scored particularly high in one area but not in others. We considered this to be a possible "leading relevance indicator" for that company or organization.

We also looked for companies that had comparatively high cumulative scores (the sum of all votes cast on all measures) to see if we could correlate corporate performance or consumer preference based on that total "relevance score."

We split the sample so that each half of the respondents assessed five of the ten categories, to keep the comparisons valid.

RELEVANCE PROFILES: OUR FINDINGS

- **Many commercial brands appear to have "leading relevance indicators"**; that is, people selected them much higher on one measure than they did on others. This was particularly true in the categories of retail, technology, and automotive companies. For example:

  o **Apple, Target, and Red Bull were distinctively "interesting and exciting."** Many more people chose them as "most interesting and exciting" than chose them for any of the other characteristics. In the technology group, two of five (41 percent) chose Apple as the "most interesting and exciting," but just one in four (27 percent) said Apple was the company they would "most want to be publicly associated with." Target was by far the "most interesting and exciting" in the retail category (54 percent), yet Target's other measures were seven to ten points lower. For Red Bull, its "interesting and exciting" score (11 percent) was five to ten times its score on other measures.

  o **The leading indicator for both Google and Walmart was "would miss most if it were gone."** This was not surprising considering the ubiquity of the brands and their dominance in their respective categories. In the technology category, 42 percent said they'd miss Google most. In retail, 32 percent said they'd miss Walmart most. For both companies, their score in other areas were more than ten points lower.

o **In the case of automotive, Ford had the most trusted profile.** More people said Ford was "closest to my values" (29 percent) than any of the other car manufacturers (next was Toyota, at 23 percent). Ford was also first (28 percent) in "most want to be publicly associated with." At the same time, Ford scored behind competitors Toyota and Honda in the area of "most interesting and exciting."

• **In the three nonprofit categories, big brands dominated.** Among nonprofit groups tested, the overwhelming favorites were the Red Cross, the American Cancer Society[3], and the National Geographic Society. However, the surprising favorite among five government agencies tested was the department most often targeted for elimination—the Department of Education.

• **High cumulative relevance scores appear to correlate with superior growth and performance despite those companies being much smaller than competitors.** It is unclear whether high relevance leads to superior growth or whether superior growth and performance lead to greater relevance. In any case, there does appear to be a clear correlation between the two.

o **Target over Walmart.** Target bested its larger rival Walmart in all five categories tested, with a relevance score of 231[4] compared with Walmart's 98. Indeed, despite being smaller than Walmart by just about every financial measure, more people said they would miss Target most if it were gone (41 percent) than would miss the world's largest retailer (32 percent).

o **Verizon over AT&T.** Similarly, Verizon bested its much larger rival AT&T on every measure despite the fact that AT&T is nearly ten times the size (in market cap). Verizon led AT&T by more than ten percentage points on every measure except one: "would miss most if they were gone." On that score, 37 percent chose Verizon and 28 percent chose AT&T. While both companies have numerous lines of business, we noted that in the wireless business, AT&T's recent reporting of fourth-quarter profits in 2011 were down 60 percent as customer growth slowed to 400,000 net new customers. During the same time period, Verizon Wireless had net additions of over 850,000 customers.[5]

o **Ford over Toyota.** Among the automobile companies, Ford had the highest relevance score (127), beating Toyota (120) and General Motors (49). Ford topped every other rival in every category except "interesting" (Toyota), despite the fact that Ford is smaller than both its Japanese rival (Toyota) and its domestic U.S. rival (General Motors). Why did Ford score so high in the areas of values and association? Was it because of its popular F150 truck and association with the slogan "Like a rock"? Could it be related to the fact that Ford was the only one of the big three

U.S. auto manufacturers that did *not* take government bailout money? We don't know. What we do
know is this. While it is smaller than its rivals, Ford
is growing. And according to reports last year 2011
Ford overtook Toyota as the United States's number-
two car maker. While Ford recently posted a near 20
percent growth in sales, Toyota's sales have been flat.

INDIVIDUAL GROUP ANALYSIS: AUTOMOTIVE

**Of the five auto companies tested, the surprising favorite
was Ford.** More people (29 percent) said Ford most closely
represented their values than any of the others. Toyota was
second. Ford was also the company that people said they
would most want to associate with (28 percent). Not only
that, of the five companies tested, more people said they'd
miss Ford if it were gone (25 percent) than any other car
manufacturer.

INDIVIDUAL GROUP ANALYSIS: RETAIL

Target dominated the five retail businesses tested. What
was stunning was the percentage gap of people who chose
Target over its much larger rival Walmart on virtually
every measure. More than twice as many people said Target was "closest to their values" than said that of Walmart
(45 percent versus 20 percent). More than four times as
many people said that Target was most interesting (54
percent versus 14 percent). Indeed, despite being a frac-

tion of Walmart's size, Target even beat the world's largest retailer on the company you would "miss most if it were gone" (41 percent to 32 percent).

INDIVIDUAL GROUP ANALYSIS: TELCO/BROADBAND

The Telco/Broadband category showcases another instance of a smaller company appearing to have a much higher relevance profile than its larger rival. Verizon outscored its rival AT&T by an average of fifteen points in four of the five areas of relevance. The closest AT&T came to Verizon was to lose by ten points in the area of "would miss most if were gone"—28 percent chose AT&T while 37 percent chose Verizon.

INDIVIDUAL GROUP ANALYSIS: TECHNOLOGY

We tested three big brands in the technology category—Google, Apple, and Microsoft—against a handful of others. Of the three, **Apple was by far the most interesting**, though it came in a distant third among those saying they would miss it most if gone (Google won that). Indeed, beyond its distinctively "interesting" quotient, Apple's relevance profile was very similar to Microsoft's, with Microsoft scoring higher than Apple in the areas of "my values" (24 percent for Microsoft and 21 percent for Apple) and preference in "doing business with" (27 percent for Microsoft and 25 percent for Apple).

INDIVIDUAL GROUP ANALYSIS: BEVERAGE

Although Coca-Cola led the pack, **the surprising second place finisher was Starbucks**, which outpaced the larger PepsiCo on every relevance dimension except "would miss [the product] most" (which was a virtual tie, with 23.6 percent choosing Starbucks and 23.8 percent choosing Pepsi).

INDIVIDUAL GROUP ANALYSIS: CRISIS NONPROFITS

We asked consumers to rate a handful of nonprofits that specialize in providing assistance in an emergency. Of those tested, the one that scored highest on four of the five relevance factors was the American Red Cross (bearing in mind that the survey respondents were Americans). Nonetheless, **Doctors Without Borders was rated most interesting** (50 percent) among the charitable organizations tested, with nearly twice as many "votes" as the American Red Cross (26 percent). Yet on measures like "closest to my own values," "want to be publicly associated with it," and "want to do business with it," Doctors Without Borders had scores similar to the American-based Salvation Army.

INDIVIDUAL GROUP ANALYSIS: HEALTH NONPROFITS

Among five large health nonprofits, **Americans showed a significant preference for the American Cancer Society**

across all dimensions. Its closest rival was the American Heart Association. The American Diabetes Society came in fourth behind March of Dimes, somewhat surprising given the fact that diabetes is a leading cause of death and that the disease is reaching epidemic status in the United States.

INDIVIDUAL GROUP ANALYSIS: ENVIRONMENTAL NONPROFITS

Of the five organizations represented, **Americans showed an overwhelming preference for the National Geographic Society**. National Geographic was particularly strong in the areas of "most interesting" (63 percent) and "would miss most" (64 percent). While the other organizations lagged, one-quarter (25 percent) of Americans said the World Wildlife Fund "most represented my values." That was more than double the number for Greenpeace (11 percent), Sierra Club (8 percent), and the Audubon Society (7 percent).

INDIVIDUAL GROUP ANALYSIS: GOVERNMENT AGENCIES

We asked people to apply the same five selections to five different federal government agencies. The agencies represented a mix of focuses, including defense, education, health, finance, and the environment. Not surprisingly, the one agency people said they would "miss most" was the Department of Defense (29 percent). However, **a surprising**

second was the Department of Education (25 percent), an agency that many people talked about eliminating. People also thought the DoD was "interesting and exciting." Nearly one third (31 percent) chose the DoD as "most interesting and exciting" among the group, though it was a statistical dead heat with the Centers for Disease Control (30 percent). Finally, people said they would most want to associate themselves with agencies that dealt with domestic issues of education and the environment. Over half (56 percent) of Americans selected either the Department of Education or the Environmental Protection Agency as the agency they would "most want to be publicly associated with."

We look forward to sharing the results of our additional surveys.

Endnotes

Executive Summary

1. Carlo DiClemente and James O. Prochaska, "Understanding How People Change Is First Step in Changing Unhealthy Behavior," American Psychological Association website, Dec. 3, 2003, http://www.apa.org/research/action/understand.aspx.
2. DiClemente and Proschaska, "Understanding How People Change Is First Step in Changing Unhealthy Behavior."

Chapter 3

1. Woody Allen, playing the part of Alvy Singer, showed this problem, literally in Technicolor, when he was introduced to Allison, played by Carol Kane, in *Annie Hall*. The exchange went like this:
   Allison: I'm in the midst of doing my thesis.
   Alvy: On what?
   Allison: Political commitment in twentieth-century literature.
   Alvy: You, you, you're like New York, Jewish, left-wing, liberal, intellectual, Central Park West, Brandeis University, the socialist summer camps and the father with the Ben Shahn drawings, right, and the strike-oriented kind of, red diaper... stop me before I make a complete imbecile of myself.
   Allison: No, that was wonderful. I love being reduced to a cultural stereotype.

Chapter 9

1. In at least one case—football—there can be an amusing benefit to irrelevance. Every year, the player picked last in the National Football League draft is dubbed "Mr. Irrelevant" and feted for up to a week. During the summer, after the draft, the

new Mr. Irrelevant (and his family) are invited to Newport Beach, California, where he is honored at a golf tournament, among other things, and receives the "Lowsman" Trophy, an obvious spoof of the Heisman Trophy (awarded to the nation's best college player). The Lowsman looks like the Heisman, but instead of carrying a football, the player is portrayed fumbling it.

2. Here is a list, which we generated in sixty seconds, of companies and industry sectors that died of irrelevance.

In the technology space: Nortel, VisiCalc, WordPerfect. Osborne and Kaypro computers and the AltaVista search engines.

Look and *Life* magazines. Borders bookstores. Encyclopedias. Maps. Pay phones. Pontiac. Oldsmobile. Photo finishing and record stores.

We bet you could generate a list just as long (and just as depressing) in the same amount of time.

Chapter 10

1. http://www.youtube.com/watch?v=LFdRFhVQwvU

Appendix

1. Numbers in parentheses represent the "value score" for that particular statement. Value scores are based on a scale of 1 to 100.

2. Professional services and high-end goods (16); personal goods (14).

3. The American Cancer Society is a client of Brodeur Partners.

4. Relevance scores are simply an aggregate of the percentages of respondents selecting that company or organization in each of the five categories. These numbers are relative and would vary considerably based on the number of businesses or organizations considered in each group.

5. Roger Cheng, "AT&T Profit Down," Dow Jones Newswires, January 27, 2011, http://tinyurl.com/5scogr2.

Index

Index

Index

Index

segmentation by relationship
  and, 60–61
thinking in, 61
values in, 62
relevance frameworks, 150–155
relevance indicators, 151,
  159–160
relevance profiles, 150
research, 97, 149–166
resistance, overcoming, 96–98
respect, 16
results, focus on, 15
rctailcrs, most relevant, 87–88,
  153, 162–163
risk reduction, 84–85
Ritz-Carlton, 66–67
Rolling Stone magazine,
  125–126

S
sales, 27
Salvation Army, 164
scenarios, 102–107
Schultz, Howard, 115–117
Schumpeter Joseph, 127
Segway personal transports, 111
self-assessment, Lake Wobegon
  effect in, 17–19
sensory appeal, 9–10, 28, 29, 59
  of hotels, 66–67
  in Relevance Egg, 62–63
services, 104–106, 138, 152
shareability, 2–3
Sheraton, 66–67
Shinseki, Eric, 121
Sierra Club, 165
situation, 45–46, 58, 72–73.
  See also circumstances

size, organizational, 151
social appeal, of retailers, 87–88
social media, 98, 133–134
society, contact and, 75
Sony Bravia, 56–58
Stanley, Thomas J., 70–71
Starbucks, 115–117, 164
strategy, 22, 23, 100–102
Swiss Army knife, 103–104

T
Target, 63, 88, 151, 159, 160–161,
  162–163
TD Bank, 70
technical products/situations,
  43–44, 145
technology, 61, 131
TED, 110, 137
temporal relevance, 59–60
thinking (functional) appeal,
  9, 10, 15, 28, 29,
  54–55, 154
  decision making and, 56–58
  of hotels, 66–67
  in Relevance Egg, 61
  values vs., 156–157
time pressures, 20, 146–147
TiVo, 49–50
Toyota, 161–162
transparency, 16
trends, studying, 129, 138
trust, 25, 27

U
underpromising and
  overdelivering, 96–97
U.S. Postal Service, 104–106

175

Index

About the Author

Andrea "Andy" Coville is CEO of Brodeur Partners, one of the world's top mid-sized communications agencies. In a quest to bring more science and sensory-based insight to the creative process she developed and refined the concept of relevance, a strategic platform for helping organizations and their brands go beyond the "buzz" and link communications to behavioral change.

For 25 years she has executed high-performing relevance campaigns for organizations in the business-to-business, consumer products and healthcare markets. Her agency's extensive client roster has included the American Cancer Society, IBM, MasterCard, Corning, Phillips, RIM (Blackberry), Bio, Vertex, 3M and GE Plastics.

After joining Brodeur in 1986 and becoming CEO in 1999, Andy diversified Brodeur Partners from a public relations firm specializing in technology to a multidisciplinary communications agency focusing on full-service communications, digital strategies, social change and business consulting. During that process she oversaw the acquisition of companies that expanded the agency's portfolio in life science, policy, online strategy and branding.

Andy has a bachelor's degree in journalism and English

literature from the University of New Hampshire. She is married to John Brodeur, co-founder of Brodeur Partners, is a mother of four children, and has a passion for non-profits and social issues that advance the well-being of children. She serves on several non-profit boards and is an avid runner and outdoor sports enthusiast.